Children of Character

Leading Your Children to Ethical Choices in Everyday Life

A Parent's Guide

Steven Carr Reuben, Ph.D.

Canter & Associates, Inc.

Contributing Writer
Mark Falstein

Editors
Marlene Canter
Carol Provisor
Barbara Schadlow

Book Design
Joyce Vario

Cover Art and Design
Richard Rossiter

© 1996 Canter & Associates, Inc.
P.O. Box 2113, Santa Monica, CA 90407-2113
800-242-4347   310-395-3221

Printed in the United States of America
First printing November 1996
01 00 99 98 97 96   10 9 8 7 6 5 4 3 2 1

Library of Congress Catalog Card Number: 96-71233
ISBN 1-57271-011-X

This book is dedicated to my stepdaughter, Gable. She has taught me more about ethical parenting than all the books I have ever read, and given me more joy, satisfaction, and fulfillment in my life than I could ever have thought possible. If all children had her kindness, her caring, her sense of empathy for all creatures large and small, and that special sweetness in her soul, the world would be a wonderful place indeed.

Acknowledgments

This book would not have been possible without the faith, support, enthusiasm and passion of Marlene Canter. For over 10 years she has responded to my own ethical and spiritual teaching with excitement, openness and a deep appreciation for the power of ideas to transform the world. Both Marlene and Lee Canter have been sources of inspiration for me, through the many powerful ideas that they have brought into the lives of children, and I am grateful for their continued support of my personal mission to inspire children to know that who they are really matters.

To Mark Falstein, who helped me transform this book into something that I hope will speak to parents in a meaningful way, and helped make my ideas so easy to absorb and communicate, I offer my deepest thanks.

To Barbara Schadlow, Carol Provisor, Toby Bernstein and the remarkable staff of Canter & Associates, who greet everyone with joy, smiles, warmth and an infectious enthusiasm for their work, thank you for welcoming me into your very special family.

And above all others, I thank my wife, Didi Carr Reuben. She is my partner, my soulmate, my daily source of strength, joy and unconditional love, and a living model of what true character is all about. Her kindness, compassion and indomitable spirit inspires every soul she touches.

Contents

 *Introduction:*

The Challenge of Raising Children of Character

From the day your child is born you must teach him to do things. Children today love luxury too much. They have detestable manners, flout authority, have no respect for their elders. They no longer rise when their parents and teachers enter the room. What kind of awful creatures will they be when they grow up?

—Socrates, 399 B.C.

Not long ago, a remarkable news story unfolded in Southern California. It was the story of Tom and Pauline Nichter and their eleven-year-old son, Jason. They had found a lost wallet on the street containing over two thousand dollars in cash, a credit card, a passport, and a plane ticket. What made the story so extraordinary was not that they had turned it all over to the police (who managed to find its rightful owner), but that Tom and Pauline were both jobless at the time, and the family was homeless and living in their car.

I watched the Nichters being interviewed on the evening news. When even the police could not help but voice their amazement, Pauline simply replied, "All we did was what we were brought up to do—to be honest." Yes, it was tempting to keep the money, Tom admitted. But he kept thinking, "What if this is all the money the person has in the world?" And Tom was painfully aware from his own recent experiences how quickly one can go from living a normal life to being out in the streets. He just couldn't keep the money.

As a result of the media coverage, people from all over the country reached into their pockets and sent the Nichters contributions of every size. Both Tom and Pauline got offers for jobs. They were helped to find an apartment, and they ended up with over $16,000 from the generosity of strangers who were moved by their act of honesty and good citizenship. As she gazed in shock at the box after box of letters and donations, Pauline Nichter laughed and said, "This is all my mother's fault."

As I watched, two thoughts occurred to me. The first was about how delighted any of us would feel as parents to be Pauline Nichter's mother—to realize the profound effect we had on our child through the moral lessons we taught. The other was about the powerful lesson eleven-year-old Jason was learning from his mom and dad. He stood there before the cameras, beaming with pride at having done the right thing. Even in the worst of circumstances, he will always have the choice to follow his parents' outstanding example in every ethical decision he makes.

As parents, we want our children to be moral, caring, and compassionate. We want them to have an inner certainty that who they are matters, what they do matters, how they talk matters, and what kind of people they become matters. Our everyday lives are filled with examples of ethical behavior. Unlike the Nichters', however, ours generally go unrecognized and unacknowledged. We miss chances to use them to inspire and educate our children. And yet our children's moral instruction is one of the most important tasks we face as parents. Simply put, the kind of children we raise will determine the kind of world in which they will live.

I've been active in the field of spiritual and moral education for over twenty years as a rabbi, a teacher, a trainer of teachers, and a child-development specialist. In all these capacities, working with parents and children of all ages, I am frequently asked such questions as, "How do you teach ethics to a child? What suggestions can you offer that will help me guide my children in making the right choices in life? Are there any simple, concrete principles and guidelines I can incorporate into my parenting to help my children become ethical human beings?"

How *do* you teach ethics to a child? How do our children learn right from wrong? How do we teach them to be the kind of people who enhance rather than diminish the quality of life in our world? How do we pass on to them the sense of morality, values, and social responsibility that is so crucial for the development of the fundamental decency needed for our society to endure? How do we instill good character?

These are some of the questions that will be answered in *Children of Character: Leading Your Children to Ethical Choices in Everyday Life.* The purpose of this book is to help you identify, simply and concretely, what you can do to help your children become ethical human beings. It can serve as a source for understanding the values you wish to pass on to your children, and as an inspirational look at how other parents have transformed everyday moments of moral mentoring into powerful lessons for living.

It is my wish to provide you with realistic guidelines and specific, concrete strategies and techniques that you will find useful in raising children in our contemporary world. On page 14 you'll find a listing of the topics we'll cover. Together we'll explore the process of working with your children to create an ethical and moral vision for their daily lives.

The Difference Between *Ethics* and *Morals*

People often confuse the words *ethical* and *moral*, and simply use them interchangeably. For the purposes of this book, I want to draw the following distinctions: *Ethical* derives from the Latin *ethicus*, meaning character, or essential quality, while *moral* is rooted in the Latin *moralis*, meaning manners or customs.

The clear implication is that behavior is ethical when it conforms to a universal, ideal standard that is a reflection of fundamental qualities of character that are "true," independent of the specific society or age in which the individual might live. Quite distinct from such a universal standard of ethics, one's behavior might still be considered moral if it merely conforms with the given standards and customs that are considered acceptable for a specific society.

The difference between ethics and morals can be understood by thinking about how our reactions to and understanding of the

What You'll Learn in this Book

This book will present you with guidelines and strategies for helping your children live an ethical, moral and responsible life. You'll learn how to:

■ Identify the specific goals you have for your children's ethical development and character building.

■ Help your children harness the power of self-esteem.

■ Model the fundamental ethical principles that have long been rooted in our culture.

■ Seize daily opportunities to teach moral lessons.

■ Follow the best current thinking on establishing guidelines for discipline at home.

■ Gain insights from experts about the different stages of children's moral development.

■ Deal with the pressures of peers and friendships.

■ Present your children with universal "rules to live by" and short, simple aphorisms that reflect the ethical traditions of our culture.

■ Take the lead in a family commitment to moral responsibility in the community and the world.

■ Communicate to your children that there is fundamental value and meaning to life.

institution of divorce has changed over the years. In days gone by, divorce was considered to be such a blot on one's reputation (especially as a woman) that people spoke of someone's divorce in the hushed tones reserved for behavior bordering on the scandalous. In those days divorce was clearly seen as a direct reflection of one's fundamental ethical character. In today's society, on the other hand, divorce has become so commonplace that it is treated in many circles almost as a normal part of the life cycle, along with birth, marriage and death.

Therefore, it would be accurate to say the *morals* of our society during the last half of the twentieth century have changed so that ending a marriage through divorce is considered unfortunate for those involved but no longer a reflection of their ethics or *character* as human beings. The ethical issues that continue to be an integral aspect of both marriage and divorce revolve around universal values such as how one fundamentally treats another human being, the integrity that is exhibited in one's life and relationships, and how personal qualities such as fairness, compassion and dignity are brought to play during the process of the divorce itself.

The distinction between an act that is ethical and one that is moral, then, revolves around the universality and timelessness of the specific behavior in question. Very often behavior that is universal (ethical) and that which in accordance with prevailing standards (moral) converge; thus the terms *ethics* and *morals* are frequently seen to be used interchangeably. The combined moral or ethical makeup of an individual is the person's *character*, which is the sum total of our focus here.

My goal in writing this book is to help parents and teachers identify the specific strategies for raising children of character, so that they will live their lives with an understanding that there are ways of behaving with friends, family and strangers in society that reflect a fundamental, universal code of ethics that cuts across race, gender, language, country of origin, economic status and age. In that way, parents can develop the tools for successfully leading their children to ethical decision making in everyday life.

 Why We Must Teach Our Children Ethics

In many ways parenting today requires tremendous courage. We face challenges that were undreamed of even a generation or two ago. The world in which our children are growing up is increasingly complex and confusing for parents, and our children's lives are radically different from those of the past. We and our children are constantly bombarded by a dizzying array of values and ethical examples from friends and family, from the media, from religious institutions and political leaders. The choices we make as parents and the choices that confront our children seem much more serious, more significant, more life-threatening than they did in ages past. Parenting today is a leap of faith into the unknown. As one parent put it, "Deciding to have a child is to have your heart walk around outside your body for the rest of your life."

Just compare these lists of problems reported by school personnel in 1940 and in 1987 (in Magid and McKevey's *High-Risk Children Without a Conscience*). In 1940 the top seven problems in schools included talking out of turn, chewing gum, making noise, running in the halls, cutting in line, dress-code infractions and loitering. By 1987 these concerns had been replaced by drug abuse, alcohol abuse, pregnancy, suicide, rape, robbery and assault!

This transformation is reflected in our social environment: the breakdown of traditional values, the culture of conspicuous consumerism, the ever-increasing rate of divorce that has produced in our culture a wider range of family configurations than ever before. All these forces have an impact on our parenting choices. Parents often tell me they feel that their control over their children is slipping away from them because of all the external influences on their children's lives. Our moral moorings have been cut adrift. We are parenting in uncharted waters.

There is an old story about two men adrift in a rowboat. All at once one of the men took out a hand drill and began to drill a hole in the bottom of the boat. Upon seeing what was going on, his partner shouted (with justifiable alarm), "Are you crazy? What are you doing? You'll sink the boat!" To which the man with the drill calmly replied, "What are you getting so upset about? I'm only drilling under *my* seat."

It happens that we're "all in the same boat." There is no way to avoid the responsibility of being interconnected with every other human being on earth. If our planet is to survive, the lessons we must teach our children all rest on this profound and essential idea.

How We Instill Ethical Expectations

Children learn ethics through their interactions with family, friends, and community. The sensitivity to others' needs that marks an ethical, responsible human being can only be developed from such contact. Only through interaction with others can children learn mutual respect, a sense of justice and fairness and an understanding of our interdependence on one another.

The primary model for children's growing sense of right and wrong behavior is, of course, the family. Children watch, learn, and imitate in one form or another the choices and actions they see their parents and siblings make. It is from their family's example that children form their sense of values and learn the behavior patterns that will guide them the rest of their lives.

Within the family system, children discover what is expected of every individual, each of whom has a unique role. Here children learn what is expected of a parent or a brother or sister. They learn how an adult is supposed to treat his or her spouse and children. They learn which behaviors are acceptable and which unacceptable, which are kept private and which discussed openly. Day after day, year after year, they absorb and learn to use thousands of items of data on how families work.

The "Internal Parent" Guides Our Choices

One important challenge we face in raising ethical children is therefore to instill in them what I like to call the "internal parent." Like Jiminy Cricket in *Pinocchio,* the internal parent is the still, small voice of conscience that whispers "yes" or "no" whenever we are confronted with ethical choices. Our job as parents is to provide our children with a substantial memory bank of hands-on personal experiences on which they can draw whenever the need to make an ethical decision arises. This will give them an expectation of their own behavior—an inner voice that whispers, "I *can make a difference. Who I am matters. What I do matters. What I say matters.* " When ethical expectations are "wired into" their self-understanding, children more easily become ethically self-regulating and ethically self-motivated.

What do I mean by these terms? "Ethically self-regulating" children are those who carry around their own internal voice of conscience. This voice is constantly giving feedback to their moral centers, letting them know whether or not a behavior they are considering is consistent with their personal sense of right and wrong. "Ethically self-motivated" children are those whose natural inclination is to treat other human beings in ways our society considers acceptable and desirable.

Children acquire these qualities primarily through living in a family environment enriched with opportunities for positive ethical decision making. In such an environment their experiences with making moral choices will produce positive, supportive feedback from adults whom they respect, admire, and love.

Ten Keys to Learning Ethical Behavior

How do we meet the challenge of raising children of character? How do we create a family environment in which our children can grow, mature, and come to understand and exhibit ethical behavior?

I have identified ten essential principles in support of this goal—ten keys for raising ethical children, each of which is a focus of a chapter in this book. At the end of each chapter is listed brief reminders of some of the techniques referred to that you can use with your children

These keys are not engraved on stone tablets; I am continually revising and refining them. But though the particulars may undergo modification, each of these keys unlocks a set of techniques and strategies for instilling moral, value-based behavior in our children.

Key #1: Set Ethical Parenting Goals

The first step in raising ethical children is to ask yourself what kind of people you want your children to grow up to be. What qualities do you want most to nurture and develop in them? How do you want them to relate to others? What activities and experiences would you have to create in order for these goals to be realized? The clearer you are about such questions, the easier it is to focus on strategies for answering them.

More important than any technique are the values you impart to your children. If we are honest with ourselves, we will admit that all values are *not* equal in our eyes. Few of us would be comfortable living in a world where values are all treated as equal, because if we embrace all values as equally valid, we are left embracing no values at all. We realize that to become "values neutral" is to abdicate our moral responsibility to establish ethical guidelines for ourselves and our children. Although we may defend the right of individuals to believe what they choose, we also believe that they must take responsibility for the effects of their values on the lives of others. In our century, we have repeatedly seen the results of ethical neutrality in the form of oppression and human suffering. To treat all values as equal we sow the seeds of moral indecision in our children, and we undermine the very moral foundation of our culture.

Most of us, however, are concerned about what kind of human beings our children will become, and will continue in this concern throughout their lives. We envision the kinds of behavior they would have to exhibit for us to feel we are successful parents and to see them as successful, competent, caring, and ethical human beings. In Key #1, you will learn how to articulate this vision and to translate it into a concrete, goal-oriented plan.

Key #2: Be a Moral Model

To raise ethical children, you must treat your children ethically. You must create an environment in which your children grow, mature, and come to understand ethical behavior by living in a family that embodies the standards that are expected of them. This is a great challenge, for it requires that an ethical consciousness pervade every aspect of our lives as parents.

Your children need you to stand for something. They need you to have clear standards and values. They need you to articulate these values through your words and, especially, through your actions. Ideally, you will consistently exhibit your ethical guidelines in a way that reinforces your children's self-worth and helps them make sense out of the world that surrounds them.

Creating a value-centered home is, of course, not dependent on the number of parents in residence, or on the kind of family structure that may exist. Whether you are married or single, straight or gay, raising your children alone or in a shared living arrangement, the essential core of your children's values must be both spelled out *and lived out* within the home environment.

Developing such an "ethical action consciousness" requires you to be clear about the values you want to teach, and to live your life in consistency with these values. Obviously, if you espouse one set of values at home and interact with the world in a way that belies these values, your children will infer that ethics and morality consist merely of slogans. Whether at home, at work or at play, in social activities or community service, it's crucial that your children see you as the kind of adult you want them to grow up to be. In Key #2, you'll learn strategies for consistently communicating in every way you can the solid ethical values that underlie your interactions with the world.

Key #3: Have Realistic, Age-Appropriate Expectations

Ethical behaviors are learned behaviors. No one comes out of the womb genetically able to make moral decisions. Just as physical, intellectual, and emotional skills develop over time, so the ability to achieve ethical insights come to children over a period of years. And just as there are discernible "stages" of learning in each of these other realms, so there are distinct stages of learning moral behavior as well.

Parents must realize that they must teach their children ethics by word and action at age-appropriate levels, or the children simply won't understand the point they are trying to make. In Key #3, you'll learn about the stages of children's ethical development and the level of moral reasoning that can be expected of them at each stage. You'll learn techniques specific to each stage for helping your children progress in a natural but guided fashion in their ability to make ethical choices.

Key #4: Demonstrate Unconditional Love

For our children to grow up able to extend their own hands to others, they need the security of feeling deep within that they are valuable, capable, competent and lovable. Only parents have the power of bestowing the gift of unconditional love upon their children. It is a spiritual inheritance within the grasp of everyone, regardless of race, religion, language, profession or financial solvency. Giving your children the blessing of unconditional love is, without question, the single most important gift you will ever give.

Remember too that your children's feeling of security and self-esteem lies not in whether you love them but in whether they *feel* loved. All the techniques I suggest throughout this book are designed to help you create an environment in which your children experience your love for them, so that they feel worthy enough as human beings to be able to pass that love along to others. It is upon feeling that we are both loved and lovable that all fundamental feelings of self-worth are ultimately based. In Key #4, you will be shown that there are opportunities daily to demonstrate your unconditional love for your children and ensure they feel both loved and lovable.

Key #5: Endow Your Children with Self-Esteem

Mahatma Gandhi was once interviewed by a Western commentator who criticized the ordinary people of India for not being more "religious" (that is, more "Christian"). Gandhi, with a sad shake of the head, replied, "My people are so poor that God can only appear to them in the form of a piece of bread." Gandhi recognized that until people's basic needs are met, there is little room for the higher issues of morality or the struggle to discover meaning and purpose in life.

Something similar can be said regarding your children. Before you can train them in the art of ethical decision-making, you must first fulfill their basic emotional and psychological needs. These are the needs for belonging, for feeling loved, accepted, and cared for, for feeling worthy of dignity and respect—in a word, for self-esteem. With the exception of essential physical needs, these requirements take precedence over everything in a child's life—intelligence, wealth, charm, beauty, even education. *No child can attend to the ethical realm until these emotional needs are met.*

This is why nurturing your children's self-esteem is one of the most precious investments in their development. Self-esteem gives children the inner strength and stability they need to reach out to the world beyond the self. In Key #5, we'll examine this all-important quality and look at specific ways in which you can instill it in your children.

Key #6: Empower Your Children with Consequences for Behavior

All too often, parents equate discipline with punishment. Nothing could be further from the truth. Discipline is the craft of teaching a child the way he or she should act. It encompasses everything you do to help your children learn to be the whole, fulfilled, ethical people you want them to become.

Naturally, there are many paths to this goal. Raising children is not an exact science. It is more like an art form, in which there are general rules and guidelines that everyone agrees are important, and a hundred different ways that individuals may interpret them. One of the most important of these guidelines concerns the distinction between *punishment* and *consequences* as a basis for discipline. In essence, discipline based on punishment represents an exercise of *power* (yours), while discipline based on consequences represents an exercise of *choice* (theirs). In Key #6, we'll explore this distinction in depth. You'll learn how to implement a disciplinary system in your home that will preserve a warm, caring environment and mutual respect, one that will guide your child in learning your values and expectations while empowering the child to make independent, thoughtful decisions.

Key #7: Look for "Teachable Moments"

The great Australian educator Sylvia Ashton-Warner coined the term "teachable moments" to refer to those times when a student is suddenly and unpredictably open, eager, reachable—teachable. The challenge for teachers is to create an environment that stimulates and encourages teachable moments, and to be aware each day that *any* action might be the one that students choose to emulate.

The same holds true for parents. We are our children's primary role models in life, whether or not we wish to be. Since we can never know in advance which of the thousands of moments we spend with our children may turn out to be memorable, the challenge is *always* to act in ways we would be proud to have our children emulate. Only then will we feel secure that any behavior of ours our children choose to copy will result in the kind of ethical behavior we wish to teach them.

Look back at your own childhood. Could the moments that had a significant impact on your ethical development have been predicted in advance? Likewise, the powerful moments that happen between us and our children simply can't be scheduled. They most often arise spontaneously. In Key #7 you'll learn ways to recognize and use these moments to teach your children ethical behavior. We'll also consider the potential of that ethics lab we call "the world" (as represented in daily life, chance happenings, TV) for providing opportunities to teach your children value-based decision making.

Key #8: Have the Kind of Friends You Want Your Children to Have

All parents wish that they could have effective veto power over their children's choice of friends, to weed out the fair-weather opportunists and "bad influences" and steer their children toward more desirable peers. We can't hand pick our children's friends, but we can influence their choice of friends. One of the most effective ways we can do this is through our own choice of friends. In Key #8, you'll learn ways to make your friendships models for your children's. You'll learn how to choose the kind of friends, and more importantly to *be* the kind of friend, that you would want your children to choose for themselves.

Key #9: Make Ethical Behavior a Family Affair

The ultimate challenge of ethical parenting is to inspire your children to see the world as if they, too, are responsible for how it all turns out. This happens only when they see themselves as intimately connected to other human beings in the great social fabric of life. This awareness must begin with the family. In Key #9, you'll find suggestions on how to make ethical behavior a family activity—within the family itself, in terms of family members' ethical responsibility to others, and in the wider community, as a means of introducing your children to the joy and satisfaction of ethical action toward others.

Key 10: Teach Your Children that Life Has Meaning

At the same time that children are becoming aware of their connection to other human beings, they must also believe in the "power of one." They must be made to recognize that their choices matter, that their life matters, that everything they do matters.

I believe that our job as parents is to communicate to our children not only the possibility that life has meaning, but the reality that they are responsible for bringing that meaning into their lives. Our job is to inspire them to see the world as filled with opportunities for greatness, for beauty, for joy, for love and blessings beyond measure. In Key #10, you'll learn strategies for inspiring your children with the conviction that there is ultimate meaning to life, and for helping them appreciate the implications of that conviction for the choices they make in their day-to-day living.

 Living As If Today Really Matters

The same standard, of living one's life as if it matters, should apply to your own choices as well as to your children's. Part of the challenge of raising children is to recognize that every day presents a new opportunity to reinforce our values. Many wise philosophers have taught us to live each day as if it were our last, to imagine each moment as if the fate of the world hung in the balance, and then to ask ourselves how we would act if that were really so. This is as true of parenting as of anything else. As you consider the ideas and techniques presented in this book, do your best to act each day with your children as if the example you set *today* will determine the kind of people they become. Live each day as if the lessons you teach today might be *the* lessons that determine whether or not they will grow up to be ethical human beings. If you can actually live each day aware of the power of your impact on your children, I am convinced that your goal of raising children of character will be tremendously easier to attain.

Children Ultimately Choose for Themselves

I opened this book with a quote from Socrates. Recently I had occasion to read a report on Socrates written by a schoolgirl. It went as follows: "Socrates was a Greek philosopher who went around giving people good advice. They poisoned him."

This little bite of truth served to deepen my own sense of humility as a presumed "expert" on parenting. It may also serve as a gentle warning to you that despite your best efforts, your control over your children's ethical development has its limits. As the Canadian psychiatrist John White reminds us in his book *Parents in Pain,* our children do not "belong" to us, but, rather, are given to us in temporary trust. It is our responsibility to watch over their development and to give them love, discipline, and moral direction. Yet regardless of our efforts, hopes, and prayers, we must remember that our children are ultimately their own persons. No matter what we do to ensure that they grow up to be ethical adults, they remain free to make their own decisions and embrace their own values. It is with this wise thought of Dr. White's that I lead you into your exploration of the Ten Keys.

Like yourselves, I am always looking for new insights. I am eager to hear of your own successes in transmitting ethical values to your children. I welcome any responses, suggestions, or personal stories that I might share with others in the future. I can be reached through the publisher of this book, Canter & Associates, P.O. Box 2113, Santa Monica, CA 90407-2113.

Leading Your Children to Ethical Choices in Everyday Life

KEY #1

Set Ethical Parenting Goals

O n a driving trip to the Grand Canyon a few summers ago, our family stopped at a restaurant for lunch. At a nearby table, I noticed a youngster of about seven waiting for his food to arrive. He was impatient, irritable and obviously very hungry; it was all he could do to stay in his chair. After what must have seemed to him an interminable wait, a hamburger and fries were placed in front of him. He began eagerly to reach for the burger, then caught himself in mid-reach. He folded his hands tightly, closed his eyes and uttered a quick, silent grace. Then his eyes popped open, and he dove into his lunch with relief and delight.

I was fascinated. Obviously this boy's parents considered prayer an important value. They had clearly focused on developing within their son a moral obligation to be thankful for his food.

Raising children of character is less a matter of using the right parenting techniques or social-skills training than a function of communicating the right *values*. Who we are and how we live are far more crucial to our children's ethical development than all the clever strategies and techniques we could ever learn from any book, including this one. This is why I believe that to raise ethical children, you must constantly remain focused on your goals for what you want them to be when they grow up.

Notice that I did not say, "what you want them to *do* when they grow up." We should be much more concerned about the kind of people our children will become than the kind of jobs they will hold. If they are the right kind of people, whatever they eventually do will simply be a reflection of who they are.

Unfortunately, most parents plan a family vacation with more care than they plan their child-rearing goals. Instead of thinking and acting in advance about our children's moral education, most of us simply react to the ethical challenges in our children's lives in a spontaneous and unprepared manner. Obviously, this approach leaves a great deal to chance. How can we translate the ethical principles that we consider important into appropriate, realistic goals that we can help our children achieve? How can we identify the values we want our children to embrace and then design experiences that support the attainment of these values?

Reflecting on Your Parenting Model

Start by considering your own childhood. Think about the occasions when you received praise from your parents. Chances are you remember being praised for success in the classroom, on the athletic field or in the social arena. Perhaps you were praised for finding a clever way to earn money or for gaining the upper hand over a competitor. But didn't your parents also praise and acknowledge you for positive ethical behavior—for exhibiting compassion and caring for another person, for being generous with your time to a friend in need, for volunteering to care for a friend's pet, for tending to the neighbors' yard while they were away on vacation, or simply for being helpful around the house?

The **"Parenting Model Worksheet" on pages 31–32** will guide you in creating a picture of the parenting models that most deeply and directly influenced your own childhood. Remember that it is our natural, unconscious tendency to imitate the models with which we grew up. It is useful for maximizing your effectiveness in making parenting decisions, therefore, to identify as clearly as you can those experiences that influenced your perceptions of what it means to be a parent. (Throughout this book, I will ask you to examine your own childhood for lessons about parenting that you learned from your own parents. It is so often the little things of life that make the biggest difference and have the most impact.)

Parenting Model Worksheet

1. List five qualities that describe your parents' parenting style (autocratic, democratic, supportive, domineering, etc.).

_____

_____

_____

_____

_____

2. List three outstanding examples of typical child-parent interactions with them.

_____

_____

_____

3. If you could have changed your parents' style in any way, what would you have changed?

_____

_____

_____

_____

_____

4. If as a child you could have told them anything you wanted them to do or say, what would it have been?

_____

_____

_____

_____

Continued on next page

continued from previous page

5. What was one of your parents' behaviors about which you told yourself as a child, "When I'm a parent, I'll *never* do that"? Do you in fact do it now?

_____

_____

_____

_____

6. What would you change about your own parenting style, if you could?

_____

_____

_____

_____

7. Recall your three most positive memories of interacting with your parents as a child. Identify the qualities they exhibited that made these experiences so positive and powerful for you.

_____

_____

_____

_____

_____

_____

_____

_____

_____

_____

Imagining Yourself As an Ideal Parent

When I used to travel the country leading the workshops I mentioned before, the greatest challenge reported by teachers was to create an environment that encouraged the best in children while getting them to do what they are supposed to do. To help teachers meet this challenge, I developed an exercise I called "The Ideal Teacher." I would ask teachers to see in their mind's eye the most influential teacher of their own life experience—anyone from kindergarten through college, as long as he or she was a positive role model. I would then ask them to list five of the qualities that they thought contributed to making that teacher so outstanding. (Never once did anyone find this an impossible task. Everyone has had at least one positive teacher, and everyone could list the qualities which to them made that teacher special.)

Next, I would have everyone share their list with the group, and write the qualities on a chalkboard, creating a composite list, based on real human beings, of all the qualities that made teachers outstanding.

After we had discussed each of the qualities, I would encourage them to write them on signs and put them up on the walls of their classrooms. In this way they would fill their teaching environment with constant reminders of the qualities they wanted to emulate and exhibit.

I share this exercise with you here because I believe that the technique also can be useful for parents. I believe that each of us has the ability to draw upon our memories of how our parents affected us to create our own picture of the Ideal Parent. By using your own life's experience as a reference point, you can identify both positive and negative examples of parenting behavior from which you can learn. (Learning what *not* to do can often be just as important as learning what *to* do.)

Do "The Ideal Parent" Exercise

Use "The Ideal Parent" exercise to create a concrete, usable picture of your Ideal Parent. It can be a wonderful activity to do with your spouse. Each of you had different parenting models, and each of you has a lifetime of valuable experiences to share with the other as a way of creating your own unique parenting team. You might want to do it as a group activity with friends or with a parenting group from your child's class.

First picture your own parents, or other significant adults or older siblings who assumed the role of parents in your early life. How would you characterize them as parents? Get a sheet of paper and list as many examples of their parenting behaviors and decisions as you can, followed by a brief (one-line) note as to the effect that each behavior had on your life. (Use the "Parenting Model Worksheet" you filled out previously to draw from.) What did your parents praise you for? Turn the memories of their praise into lessons about their values. What ethical principles did they care most about?

Now use these memories to clarify your own ethical-parenting goals. Think of what you praise your children for. As a parent, nearly everything you do is a form of teaching. Every smile you give your children, every word of encouragement, teaches them what is important to you about who they are and how they behave. The more conscious you are about the lessons you teach them, the more effectively these lessons will reinforce your values. **"My Ethical Parenting Goals" worksheet on pages 36–37** will help in identifying your most important values and the experiences through which you want to teach those values to your children.

Begin by identifying your own values. What *are* your values? If you were designing a program, a class, or curriculum in ethical behavior (and you are!), what would you consider to be the most important principles of that program? What values, years from now, would give you the most satisfaction to observe in your children?

For example: Norman Vincent Peale, the author and spiritual leader, named these as his seven core values: honesty, courage, enthusiasm, service, faith, hope, and love. William Bennett, former cabinet official and author of *The Book of Virtues*, listed ten: self-discipline, compassion, responsibility, friendship, work, courage, perseverance, honesty, loyalty, and faith.

Make a list of the values you consider important and write them down on the worksheet. Of course your own list may be different from either Peale's or Bennett's, and there may well be more than ten values that you wish to pass on to your children. But be careful not to choose so many as to make the process unwieldy—when my wife and I first did this exercise, we came up with a list of sixty!

Next, take a long, careful look at the list and select from it your *core* values—the ones that are most important to you; the ones you want to be sure to pass along to your children. Write your core values on the worksheet; these core values form your ethical parenting goals. Copy them onto a large sheet of paper and post them in a prominent place in your home, where you and your children will see them every day and be continually reminded, "These are the core values of our family. These are the things we think are really important."

Now, imagine your child as the ethically perfect adult you'd like her to grow up to be, consistently practicing all the values on your list. Think about it with "20-20 hindsight." We all know about 20-20 hindsight: "Well, gee, if I only knew then what I know now, I would have..." Ask yourself the question: "If this is the adult I wanted my child to be, with all those values I wanted her to incorporate into her life, what experiences and activities did I provide or offer her that led her to embrace these values?"

Thinking with 20-20 hindsight gives you a road map for raising your child. What kinds of family activities will help you and your child reach these goals? What forms of enrichment? What books, movies, cultural events, vacations? What experiences in the community, helping other people and reinforcing caring behavior, would you have to provide in order for your child to grow up to be the responsible, moral adult with the kind of character you envision?

These experiences need not be complicated or expensive. A family picnic, for example, can be a value-reinforcing experience.

My Ethical-Parenting Goals

My Values

_____

_____

_____

_____

_____

_____

_____

_____

_____

_____

_____

_____

_____

_____

_____

_____

_____

_____

_____

_____

_____

_____

_____

_____

My Core Values

_____

_____

_____

_____

_____

_____

_____

_____

_____

_____

Family Experiences and Activities to Support My Core Values

_____

_____

_____

_____

_____

_____

_____

_____

_____

_____

_____

_____

_____

_____

_____

Have your child invite a friend, and bring along friends of your own. This will reinforce the values of friendship, sharing, and family itself.

Or, consider a day at the zoo. Let your child ask a volunteer how various animals are fed, what they do in bad weather, and how they are cared for when they get sick. This experience will reinforce the values of compassion for living creatures, responsibility, perseverance, and even love.

And do not neglect social-service agencies. Volunteering for your family to spend an afternoon helping out at a food pantry, homeless shelter, children's hospital, or other such institution can reinforce many important values.

Use these suggestions and your 20-20 hindsight to plan an appropriate array of experiences for your child, and write your plans in the space provided on the worksheet.

When Partners Have Different Values, Team Up

Unless you're a single parent, you and your partner may have differing, perhaps even conflicting values. This is a conflict that must be resolved. Children need a clear understanding of what is expected of them in all aspects of their lives. In particular, they need a consistent set of ethical guidelines. When parents appear confused, kids become confused. When mixed messages lead a child to be confused about which parent is "right," it stands to reason that the child will be mixed up too. When one parent acts with concern, sensitivity and compassion toward the homeless, for example, while the other speaks of them as "low-lifes" who should be run out of town, the child will suffer from an ethical identity crisis.

The ideal approach to ethical parenting is a team approach. Finding agreement is a loving gift you can give your children. There are a few relatively simple steps you can take to help you arrive at a program of agreed-upon values.

First, sit down and have a conference. Make individual lists of your core values. Compare your lists and edit them into a third document that enumerates the points about which you agree. This will leave for discussion and resolution only those on which you disagree. Then, if the two of you cannot reach agreement on them, enlist a counselor, clergyperson, or friend to act as mediator.

If you are divorced, do your best to have such a conference with your ex-spouse. I realize that this may be impossible, given the intensity of feelings leading to and following the breakup of a marriage; but ideally, the child's welfare ought to outweigh individual hurts and angers and give both sides a common focus. Parenting must be a partnership among all parents—whether there are one, two, three, or four involved in your children's family sphere. Their emotional, spiritual and moral upbringing will be strengthened to the degree that you can function as a team.

Presenting a clear and consistent message gives your children emotional security—as well as taking away from them the option of playing one parent against the other. Children need to know that their family has a clearly articulated set of values on which they can rely. In the ever-changing world of childhood, this moral constancy is one of the most important gifts you can give them.

Teaching by Example

How can you maximize your chances of passing your values along to your children? What steps can you take to make your goals theirs?

Think again for a moment of your own childhood. Focus on one of the values that your parents passed on to you. You can probably think of many—be nice, have integrity, tell the truth—but for now, think of the *one* outstanding value your parents taught you.

Now consider *how* your parents taught you that value. When I ask people to do this in my workshops for parents and teachers, I get the same response one hundred percent of the time: *by example.*

Everything you do teaches by example. You are constantly demonstrating to your children your values, goals, and ethical standards by your daily behavior—whether you want to or not. The most effective way of passing along your ethical goals to your children is simply to *live* them. (In later chapters, we'll take a close look at how you can model the values you want your children to emulate, and how your own ethical standards can serve as lessons for their own developing sense of moral responsibility.)

Use the Power of Positive Reinforcement

Another way to keep your children focused on your values is to practice *positive reinforcement.* This technique is based on the simple idea that if we want people to act in a certain way, we will achieve the best results if we reward them for the behavior we desire. We practice forms of positive reinforcement throughout our lives. Babies stop crying after a parent has complied with their desired behavior—feeding, cuddling, or changing a messy diaper. Adolescents master the appropriate cues, verbal and non-verbal, that encourage or discourage particular behaviors from their dates. We all know that to achieve the behavioral results we desire from those around us, we need to apply appropriate positive reinforcement.

The same rule applies when it comes to raising ethical children. We are trying to inculcate our children with an almost automatic ethical response to whatever real-life situations might arise. We want the same satisfaction as Pauline Nichter's mother, knowing that we have raised a child to whom honesty, justice and compassion (or whatever our core values may be) are second nature.

To do this, you need to be in a frame of mind where instead of watching out for your children's transgressions against your parental "commandments," you *catch them in the act of doing something right.* This is a phrase coined by Kenneth Blanchard and Spencer Johnson in *The One-Minute Manager,* but it applies to parents every bit as much as to business executives.

Imagine the impact on your children's ethical behavior if instead of only noticing what they do wrong, you actively searched for and recognized the things they do well, the characteristics they exhibit of which you are proud, the acts of kindness, caring, and honesty that reflect the quality of their character. Positive reinforcement is *the single best way* to implant in a child's psyche the importance of experiencing a particular behavior as an integral part of his being.

Children Need to Be Acknowledged

Keep in mind that children will get attention in any way they can. All children seek acknowledgment; it is a fundamental human need. If they can't get it in a positive way, they will be sure to get it by acting out in a negative way. Either way, the end result is attention from, and acknowledgment by, adults. Their behavior, and the adults' response, lets them know on a basic, instinctual level that their existence is recognized in the world.

As sad as it seems, when children act out negatively, they are sending the message that they would rather get negative acknowledgment than none at all. Part of our job as parents is to direct their behavior toward positive, socially acceptable paths so that their behavior and actions reinforce an internal belief that their essential nature is one of goodness and value.

Your children are already acting in ethically appropriate ways. The challenge is to recognize and acknowledge when they act in accordance with your values, and to reward them when they do. It follows that when they need attention, they will be more likely to seek it by acting in a way that will meet with your approval.

Watch What You Praise

Praise is the currency of positive reinforcement, the number-one reward you can give your child. It is therefore necessary to be aware of *what* behaviors you praise. Unless you are consciously focused on your ethical-parenting goals, it is much easier to give praise for getting an A on a test or for hitting a home run. These may be the headlines of your child's life, but values are expressed in the fine print. Praise your children for the small, daily fine-print items: returning a toy that another child left at your house, going out of their way to show a kindness to a younger sibling, offering to visit a bedridden great aunt. You don't have to proclaim it on a billboard, but do keep in mind that every incident of praise reinforces the behavior you are praising.

How to Be "A Good Enough Parent"

It is important for you to have appropriate, realistic goals and expectations for yourself as well as for your children. A "perfect parent" does not exist. All that's necessary is to be "a good enough parent," as the renowned child psychiatrist and author Bruno Bettelheim put it. If you feel that you must hold yourself to an idealized standard, never make mistakes, always remain calm, and always respond correctly to whatever your children may say or do, you are headed for parental self-destruction and emotional disaster. Being "good enough" is an achievable goal, one that won't drive you crazy in pursuit of an impossible dream.

Spend "Quality Time" with Your Children

One thing you can do is simply to give your children the gift of time. In a famous 1986 study by the University of Michigan Institute of Social Research, mothers who worked outside the home were found to spend an average of only eleven minutes daily in exclusive play or teaching time (called "quality time") with their children on weekdays, and about thirty minutes on weekends. The data for fathers were only eight and fourteen minutes respectively. Even mothers who did not work outside the home devoted an average of only thirteen minutes per day to quality time to their kids.

You can imagine what an impossible task parents set for themselves if they are willing to commit such a limited amount of time to their children's upbringing. Time is one of the most precious gifts you can give another human being. Without it, successful parenting takes on all the certainty of a crap game. You are leaving the success of your childrearing to mere chance.

If this were what you wanted, you wouldn't be reading this book. Since you are the kind of parent who cares deeply about your children and who is committed to helping them become ethical human beings, make a point of spending quality time with them. It is next to impossible to convey your values to them if you do not.

Listen with Your Eyes

One of the most important ways of winning your children's respect for your values is through the simple act of listening. We know from our own experience that when people listen to what we have to say, it sends us the undeniable message that we are worthwhile, important, and valuable in their eyes.

Consider the story of the child who came home one day to find his father busy in the kitchen. The child began to relate the story of his adventures at school that day. From time to time, without looking up from his dinner preparations, the father would nod and grunt, "Uh-huh." Finally, with a note of irritation, the boy said to his father, "You aren't listening to me!"

"Of course I'm listening to you," the father responded.

"But Daddy," the boy said, "you're not listening with your *eyes*."

That's our challenge: to listen with our eyes. There is no substitute for the validation we give our children through the simple act of *looking* at them as we speak. It communicates more directly than almost anything else we can do that we find them worthy of attention. It is a simple, powerful way of conveying love and respect, of giving those we love the message that they are important to us, of telling them that there is nothing we would rather be doing than being right there with them.

This advice may seem simplistic. With all the sophisticated research that has been done in child development and education, here I am simply telling you to "listen with your eyes"?

In fact, I cannot emphasize enough how important this is. If you want your children to feel that your values count for something, they must feel that what they have to say counts for something too. Give them your attention, your eyes firmly fixed on them, and they will truly feel worthwhile, valued, and loved.

Be a Visionary Guide

Another powerful technique for your children's moral development is encouraging them to create in their minds a vision of the ethical human being they wish to become. It helps them form a general picture of what an ethical person looks, talks, and acts like; and to personalize that vision as a positive model of the adult they want to grow up to be.

"For as one thinks, so shall his end be," says the Biblical Book of Proverbs. This thought in one form or other is the motto of countless psychologists, self-help groups, and motivational speakers. In every era, in every culture, thinkers and spiritual people have recognized the fundamental truth that we become what we think about. Indeed, the power of thought to help us internalize the qualities we wish to emulate and the goals we wish to achieve has been a driving force behind successful men and women in all fields of endeavor.

The challenge of successful ethical parenting is to help guide your children along this path of positive self-imaging, so that their internal vision represents the highest, noblest picture of an ethical self that they can create. Refer to the **"Positive Self-Image Activities" on page 45** for several simple ideas for inspiring your children to think about this ethical vision of themselves.

Positive Self-Image Activities for Your Children

Help your children create a vision of the ethical person they would like to be.

■ Suggest that your child draw a picture of how a "good person" acts toward others: If he were "Mr. Compassion," how would he act toward his friends? Toward his teacher? Toward someone he doesn't like? Toward an animal he found lost in the street?

■ Have your child write or present in drawings a story called "A Day in the Life of Me the Great"—the most ethical person in the world. Have her use her own name in the story, and talk to her as if she already were that person. Put the story or pictures on the wall or refrigerator and review it with your child from time to time. (You may want to repeat this exercise every month, focusing on a different value or quality each time.)

■ Create an ongoing "values mirror" of your child. Draw an outline of the child on butcher paper. Fill it in with material illustrating your core values that you and the child gather from newspapers and magazines. Hang this ethical self-portrait on a wall.

Teach Your Children the Importance of Choice

Every day of our lives, we make decisions that help determine our character. Every ethical choice we make becomes part of our understanding of our essential nature. This is why achieving your ethical-parenting goals depends on communicating to your children that all behavior involves choices, and that the quality of their lives is ultimately dependent on the quality of their choices.

I cannot overemphasize the importance of teaching your children the impact their daily choices have on their lives. Choice determines not only who we are, but whether we live to see tomorrow. The issue of drug abuse, for example, isn't so much an issue of education as an issue of choice. If it were simply a matter of education, no one would smoke cigarettes any more. The first Surgeon-General's report linking smoking with cancer and other life-threatening diseases came out more than thirty years ago. We've all seen the statistics: In a typical two-week period, according to one study (in Zig Ziglar's *Raising Positive Kids in a Negative World*), more Americans die as a direct result of smoking than die of AIDS in the course of a year—yet people continue to smoke.

The same applies to alcohol and drugs. Nearly every school-age child in America is aware of their dangers. Yet according to the University of Michigan Institute for Social Research, eighty-seven percent of America's high-school seniors in 1993 were at least occasional users of alcohol, and over thirty-five percent used marijuana or other illegal drugs. A *Dallas Morning News* article (March 18, 1988) reported that approximately 100,000 ten- and eleven-year-olds got drunk at least once every week.

With the reality behind such statistics facing us every day in our communities and in our own families, it shouldn't be hard to understand why I am making such a strong case for teaching your children about the impact of choice. Teaching them how to make responsible ethical decisions involves training them from the earliest years that all behavior involves choices. In fact, implied in those frightening data is the lesson that the choices themselves determine whether our actions are ethical or not.

The recognition that each of us has an impact on our world through the choices we make is a crucial component of ethical behavior. Without choice, ethics would be irrelevant. No one holds others responsible for their behavior if they are without choice. It is through the choices we make daily in our interactions with others that we define ourselves as ethical human beings.

That is why we parents must create opportunities for our children to recognize their ability to make choices and to understand and experience the consequences of their choices. Even very young children can be given a wide range of choices: "Do you want to wear the blue shirt or the green shirt today?" "Do you want the banana or the apple?" "Do you want to eat it now or later?" These age-appropriate decisions give children needed training in making the daily decisions that affect their lives.

Giving children choices empowers them to feel that they have some control over themselves and their environment. You start with simple and harmless choices, and as they grow older, they will be competent to make more difficult choices—the choice of friends, the choice of actions, the choice of behavior toward others.

Empowering your children to make positive, appropriate decisions and to understand the consequences of their decisions also adds to their growing sense of place in the larger social world. When children grow up with the habit of choice, they learn to respect the right of others to make choices as well. This realization strengthens their feeling of being connected to the lives of other human beings, and their understanding that each of us is both an independent and an interdependent being.

The World Children Dream About

After the civil disturbances in Los Angeles in 1992, the city's School District and Cultural Affairs Department worked with several schools and their children's choirs to produce a musical video called "The World I Dream About." It was an attempt to give children whose emotional lives were devastated by the daily threat of violence the opportunity to express their hopes and dreams of a world in which all children can grow up in a society that encourages their talents and abilities, nurtures their sense of self-worth, and inspires them to fulfill themselves in every way.

I close this chapter with these thoughts because the need for such a dream is not restricted to a riot-torn city. Fortunately, most of us cannot relate personally to the cartoon that ran in the *Los Angeles Times* after the disturbances, depicting two African-American children sitting on the steps of a run-down inner-city home. One child is turning to the other and asking, "What do you want to be if you grow up?" Most of us have the luxury of assuming that our children will grow up physically safe and protected, yet too many of us continue to focus on what our children will grow up to do rather than the kind of person they will grow up to be.

That's why we need to set ethical-parenting goals for ourselves and for our children. I dream of the day when children are praised for being kind, considerate, caring human beings, and not only for their academic, athletic, or financial achievements. That, to me, is a world that is truly worth dreaming about.

How to Set Ethical Parenting Goals and Help Your Children Achieve Them

■ Recognize that values are the basis of ethical behavior.

■ Identify the values that are most important to you, and design experiences for your children that will reinforce those values.

■ Always give your children positive reinforcement for behavior that supports your values.

■ Give your children time, attention, and visionary guidance.

■ Create opportunities for your children to make meaningful choices.

■ Live your life as the kind of adult you want your children to grow up to be.

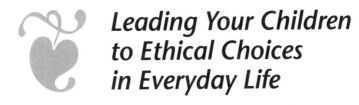

*Leading Your Children
to Ethical Choices
in Everyday Life*

KEY #2

Be a Moral Model

"Children have never been good at listening to their elders," James Baldwin wrote, "but they have never failed to imitate them." This is a reality that no parent can evade. Our children learn by watching, not by listening to us preach (and being a rabbi, I ought to know!) What you *say* about values has a minuscule effect compared with the sledgehammer impact of your actions. How you act, what you do, what you are—*these* are the lessons that you teach your children, day in and day out.

Being a role model for our children is not an option. It is a fact of life. We *are* a model for our children's behavior, day after day, every day, so we must be very careful about what we model. In this book I have listed moral modeling as the second key to raising ethical children, but I might just as well have listed it as number one. Modeling ethical behavior for your children transcends every other lesson we could ever hope to teach them.

We learn our ethical lessons by example, by watching how our parents and other adult role models live and interact with others. This is not to say that words and moral sayings are unimportant. They reinforce your behavior with a framework of ideas that sets it in a larger context. But verbal lessons are important only to the degree that they are consistent with the ways your children see you behave. They can only remind children of the behavior they should be experiencing through your everyday actions.

The most powerful lessons I learned from my parents came from watching them live their lives in accordance with the values they taught. Walking precincts with my mother in support of candidates she supported. Traveling with my father on a Boy Scout trip to Mexico to bring clothes and food to impoverished youth. Watching both of them give their time and money to causes, organizations, and individuals who brought health care, education, and greater dignity and self-worth to people suffering from poverty and abuse. These lessons taught me about my human responsibility to act in accordance with a clear set of ethical standards.

Doing the Right Thing

When it comes to raising our children, we can't get away with much. *Children notice,* even when we think they're not paying attention—even when they're in another room! They know when your actions don't measure up to your words. This is why "Do as I say, not as I do" does us no good. It teaches them that it is okay to be hypocritical. If this is how they experience their parents, their source of moral authority, why should they expect anything different from the great wide world?

That is why being a moral model is such a responsibility, all the time. When we talk to our spouse, when we talk on the phone, when we talk about or interact with family and friends, we must always be sure that we are living according to the values we want our children to respect and emulate.

An example of moral modeling in my own family was an incident that happened several years ago when my wife and daughter were getting out of their car at a shopping mall. When my daughter, Gable, opened the door, she accidentally banged it into another car, leaving a small mark. My wife, Didi, immediately got out a pad of paper and started writing a note. When Gable asked her what she was doing, she replied, "I'm leaving a note for the owner of the other car so that he or she can get in touch with me."

Gable said, "But no one saw us. Why don't we just leave? No one will know."

Didi answered, "What do you mean, no one will know? The two most important people will know—you and I. Always remember the saying, 'What goes around comes around.' This is simply the right thing to do."

The truth was that Gable really didn't understand why they couldn't just go into the mall and forget about it. She was eight years old at the time, and her response was appropriate to the stage of her developmental thinking. But her mother's behavior had implanted in her mind the idea of "doing the right thing."

What was truly fortuitous was that about a month later, Didi was leaving another shopping mall with Gable and found a note on the windshield from a stranger who had dinged *her* car. Gable immediately exclaimed, "Look, Mommy, you were right! It came back to us already!"

Now, I can hardly promise that you will have such direct one-to-one payback for the ethical acts you perform! I can assure you, however, that one way or another, modeling ethical behavior for your children will pay off in their own behavior. In that sense, what goes around can practically be guaranteed to come around.

How to Make Ethical Behavior Ordinary Behavior

There are hundreds of ways to illustrate your values, to show your children by example the kind of adult you want them to become. What you want your children to learn is that we make choices about ethical behavior every day. It is not something that happens self-consciously, or only under duress. To be fundamental to your children's character, it must be integrated into their lives until it seems ordinary to them. It must be found in simple gestures, casual remarks, and almost unconscious acts of kindness or concern that reflect a fundamental ethical attitude toward family members, friends, and strangers:

- You are a moral model every time you go out of your way to respond to the needs of others.
- You are a moral model when you give up part of your weekend to visit a relative in a nursing home.

- You are a moral model when you listen compassionately and without judgment to a neighbor who is dealing with difficult life decisions.
- You are a moral model when, instead of grabbing a parking space that another driver has clearly been waiting for, you allow her to have it.
- You are a moral model every time you show kindness to your children.

Kindness Is a Basic Moral Value

An ancient proverb teaches us that "The highest form of wisdom is kindness." After many years counseling individuals and families and observing parents trying to convey moral values to their children against the countervailing examples of our look-out-for-number-one society, I am more convinced than ever of the power of kindness to shape people's lives. Showing kindness to other people, especially to your own children on a consistent basis, teaches them a powerful lesson. It communicates on a direct emotional level that you believe in the inherent worth and value of another person. It demonstrates to your children that positive ethical values can be expressed in an everyday context.

Mean What You Say

Integrity is another key value that you must practice on an everyday basis. Unless you establish yourself as an example of trust, it becomes much more difficult to raise your children to be ethical adults. We all want our children to grow up to be the kind of people that others can rely on. This is a behavior they must learn from you—again, not by what you preach, but by the way you live your life every day. Parents *must* be trustworthy. When you fail to model integrity, you are teaching your children to lie.

There used to be a saying in the airline business that a passenger who sees that the ashtrays are dirty will assume that the engines are in equally ill repair. We all generalize from the particular. We take our own personal, narrow-focus experiences and assume that the rest of the world is a larger reflection of them.

So it is with our children. If you make promises idly and don't follow through, you lose credibility with your children. If you make promises without intending to fulfill them, out of frustration with the demands of the moment, you are demonstrating to your children that they can't trust you. They may not recall the exact promises broken (then again, they very well may!), but you can be sure they will conclude that your word can't be counted on. If they can't count on your word in inconsequential matters, how can you be credible when it comes to more serious matters?

Integrity and trust come in many forms, but they all have to do with keeping commitments. When your children grow up knowing that when you tell them you'll be home at ten, they can count on you to be there if they wake up at eleven, it is easier for them to understand why you expect the same behavior when they begin to go out as teenagers. Children either learn that a person's word is important, or they learn that it shouldn't be taken all that seriously. If the latter is what they experience as children, they may have difficulty keeping their commitments as adults.

Show Your Children Dignity and Respect

Moral modeling also applies to issues of personal dignity and respect. If you want your children to respect the worth and value of other human beings, you must demonstrate your respect for their own worth and value. One simple way to do this is by creating a positive, open climate for discussion of ideas and moral issues.

Even when children are very young, you want them to feel free to discuss difficult ethical questions. If you respond to statements with which you disagree by interjecting "That's stupid," or to naive statements by laughing dismissively, you are teaching them that it's okay to assault the dignity of others—and that it's safer not to offer opinions in the first place.

No one likes to feel stupid. Few of us are willing repeatedly to put ourselves in situations in which our self-respect is under attack. That is why it is important to create within your family an emotionally safe environment for discussing ethical issues. The more children struggle aloud with others about these issues, the more clearly they can define and redefine their values.

This is the only healthy way that children can reach a clear position on moral questions. If they don't feel safe discussing them with you, they will likely turn to their peers and *their* parents for the working out of tough ethical choices—choices involving such issues as drugs, sex, abortion, relationships, personal freedom. Or they will turn to the movies, TV, and popular music. It is much more desirable for you to create an open, non-judgmental home environment in which your children know that any opinion they might express will be listened to with respect and regarded as serious and thoughtful.

Some families use the dinner table as a forum for bringing up the ethical issues that affect their lives. Others use news stories or "Dear Abby" columns as nonthreatening grist for the ethical-dilemmas mill. In discussing such real-life dramas, you allow your children to be co-partners with the adults in the process of moral discovery and decision making.

You must believe that you have an important ethical message to pass on to your children. Otherwise, you abdicate your responsibility as a parent and leave your children's moral modeling to others. Yet you must also make sure your family is an island of love and support, a safe place for your children to grapple with the moral questions that affect their lives. Only if you model respect for their thoughts and feelings as developing ethical human beings will they come to respect your values.

Involve Your Children in Family Decisions

As a self-contained "mini-society," your family can provide a laboratory for ethical decision-making in the wider social world. One way to accomplish this goal is to create a model for setting family rules that is more democratic than the traditional system in which all rules are made by the parents.

Obviously, some issues must be left to parental discretion. Questions of health and safety (including rules about smoking and alcohol consumption), decisions about when children must be home in the evening, and rules about which privileges must wait until chores and homework are done should not be open to democratization. Nevertheless, there are many areas of family life in which your children can appropriately participate in making rules, such as:

- Recreation time and after-school activities.
- Study hours, and study environment (for example, whether they may study with music playing).
- Decisions about meals.
- What they may wear to school.
- Delegation of household chores.
- How they may spend their own money.
- Attendance at religious services.
- Overnight sleepovers with friends.

By bringing your children into the decision-making process, you acknowledge them as individuals with their own thoughts and concerns. You model respect and trust. You'll discover how much easier it is to get them to follow the rules when they have had a hand in creating them. You'll face far fewer challenges to your parental authority. You may even be surprised at how thoughtful and appropriate your children's ideas turn out to be.

Many families have regular meetings to discuss issues, review rules, assign responsibilities, and plan future activities. These meetings may be held weekly, monthly, or at whatever interval works best. They need not have a set format; every family can work out a method that suits its needs, issues, and personalities. The key is to encourage maximum participation so that all family members feel that their concerns are being heard and considered.

Through such meetings, children can learn that they are important within the family system, and adults *and* children can learn lessons in conflict resolution, negotiation, and compromise.

One aspect of this family approach to rules often encounters resistance—from parents! When rules are openly and democratically arrived at, parents are bound to abide by them as much as children. If the whole family is involved in the setting up of rules about chores that must be done, for example, or about how many hours of television may be watched during the week, both adults *and* children must respect the decisions. When you honor these joint decisions, you model both integrity and respect.

The Foundation of Our Moral Value System

I have my own obvious bias on this topic. I had a strong religious upbringing, and I work in and through religious institutions. Yet it has seemed clear to me year after year that the individuals with the strongest sense of ethics, the people best equipped to meet the complex moral challenges of today, are those with strong spiritual and religious foundations. Therefore I believe that it is desirable to model ethical behavior from a religious perspective and to pass along such a perspective to your children as part of a shared tradition.

I believe that the foundation of morality rests with a transcendent Source or Power, which in our language we call "God." I believe that this Power lies beyond the full understanding of human beings, and yet is the ultimate source of the values that form our culture's ethical system. I believe that it is through the recognition of this moral authority in the universe that we can assert that some behaviors are right and others are wrong.

We call this moral system "ethical monotheism," or "Judeo-Christian ethics." But even if one doesn't believe in God, the Judeo-Christian tradition, or any religion at all, we are committed to standards of ethics which, in our culture, derive from this tradition. Kindness, compassion, integrity, justice, humility, personal growth, respect, love, any and all of the values that are likely to appear on your "core list," come to us through this commonly acknowledged ethical system.

I believe that it is much easier to raise ethical children when you are personally grounded in the ethical principles of the Judeo-Christian tradition. It doesn't matter so much which particular religion you embrace, only that you embrace *a* religion. Ultimately, regardless of any religion's claim to have the "right answer" or to be in special contact with God's will, all religions have the same goal: to create ethically committed human beings. All religions teach the sacredness of life and the universality of the human community. I believe that the basis of all rituals, theologies, religious laws, and sacred texts is to help us be the best human beings that we can possibly be, so that we can create an earth filled with justice, compassion, and Godliness.

Demonstrating Moral Courage

Being a parent today requires moral courage—the inner strength to stand up against those forces in society that seem to denigrate or disparage the values you hold important. It takes moral courage to accept the awesome responsibility of raising children in what so often appears to be an unhealthy, unethical moral environment. It takes moral courage to believe in yourself and your standards of behavior, to believe that there are fundamental values that transcend time and popularity, to believe passionately that these values are worth modeling for your children.

We demonstrate moral courage when:

- We insist on telling the truth to a friend, even though it may be uncomfortable to do so.
- We speak out against a school board bent on censoring great literature in the name of a current fad.

■ We write to a newspaper to publicly compliment the editors for their willingness to run a story on a controversial moral subject.

We are most effective as models of moral courage when we make such acts an everyday part of our lives. Studies of courageous, unselfish behavior in Nazi-occupied Europe have shown that most individuals who risked their lives to protect others didn't think they were doing anything extraordinary. People who hid others in their homes to save them from the death camps, who provided food and clothing to the oppressed, or who set up secret schools, consistently reflected that they simply couldn't have imagined acting in any other way. For them, their behavior was simply an expression of what it means to be a human being living among other human beings who share similar needs, hopes, and dreams.

Such individuals learned that this behavior was "ethical" from compassionate and caring priests and pastors. But they learned that such behavior was "ordinary" from their home life—from how their own parents and how they treated other people.

The Power of Parental Example

Time and again, the testimony of caring, ethical people underscores the fundamental truth of the power of parental example: If you demonstrate good character, so shall your children. It is crucial to be aware of the opportunities you have to reinforce your children's ethical behavior by your actions.

This is why it is so important to act each day in ways you want your children to emulate. No, you should not expect to be perfect, or to make the right decision every time. But you can develop an "ethical-action consciousness" by following this rule of thumb: Whenever you are confronted with an ethical decision, ask yourself how you would want your child to act in the same situation. Most often, you will know immediately which choice is best for you.

We cannot always know what our children experience outside our homes, but we do have some measure of control over what happens inside. Our homes must be laboratories for ethical behavior as well as sanctuaries of safety and love. What goes around will indeed come around: When children know what it feels like on a daily basis to be shown kindness, trust, justice, and respect, they will come to express and exhibit such qualities as a matter of course. When you create an ethical context for their lives, they will be unable to imagine living any other way.

How to Model Ethical Behavior

■ Recognize that you are your children's primary role model, and that your children will know when your actions do not measure up to your words.

■ Demonstrate your core values in your everyday actions.

■ Show your children kindness and integrity on a daily basis.

■ Treat your children with dignity and respect.

■ Observe standards of behavior that are grounded in the spiritual traditions of our culture.

■ Be courageous in standing up for your values.

■ Whenever you are confronted with an ethical decision, ask yourself how you would want your child to act in the same situation.

*Leading Your Children
to Ethical Choices
in Everyday Life*

KEY #3

Have Realistic, Age- Appropriate Expectations

There is a story about a three-year-old boy who was sitting in the back seat of the family car eating an apple. "Daddy," the boy asked, "why is my apple turning brown?"

"Because," his father explained, "after the skin was cut off, the meat of apple came into contact with the air. This caused it to oxidize, changing its molecular structure, with the result that the apple turned a different color."

A long silence followed. Then a small voice came softly from the back seat: "Daddy, are you talking to *me?*"

Every person goes through recognizable stages of mental and physical development over the course of a lifetime. No one would expect to teach a three-year-old to master the principles of organic chemistry or free-throw shooting. We understand that a preschooler's attributes and abilities are worlds apart from those of an adolescent. We expect our children to pass through various stages, and we hardly give it a second thought when they do.

It has only become clear in recent decades, however, that children pass through distinct stages of moral development as well. There are differences of opinion among psychologists about the specifics of these stages and the key factors involved in a child's moving smoothly from one to the next, but there is universal agreement that children progress in their moral reasoning in the same gradual fashion as they master physical and intellectual skills. Dr. Lawrence Kohlberg, for example, described the process as one of passage from "premorality" through "conventional morality" to "principled morality." On the next page is an overview of the stages children pass through as they develop moral reasoning.

Stages of Children's Moral Development

Stage One	Might Makes Right	*Power belongs to the older and stronger*
Stage Two	An Eye for an Eye	*Take equal and exact revenge*
Stage Three	The Moral Mirror of Others	*Look for approval*
Stage Four	Internalized Ethical Self-Image	*Temper justice with compassion*
Stage Five	Social Obligation	*Participate in a larger, more complex group*
Stage Six	Spiritual Democracy and Personal Responsibility	*Respect the rights of others*

Bringing our children to the level of principled morality is the result of a natural progression of role-modeling, shared experiences, thoughtful talks, and positive discipline. There are no simple step-by-step directions that will guarantee our success. The point, however, is that while ethical behaviors are learned behaviors, they also reflect natural tendencies. There are guidelines we can follow that can increase our chances of success by taking these tendencies into account. If we help our children's ethical reasoning to progress in a guided fashion, they are more likely to arrive appropriately at each successive stage of moral development. Let's now take a look at each of these stages and how children typically progress from one to the next, and see what we can do to guide them along.

Stage One: Might Makes Right

The lowest level of moral reasoning could be called the "might-makes-right" level. At this stage, the only motivation for ethical behavior is staying out of trouble with adults, who are perceived as all-powerful and generally all-knowing. In a child of four or five, this kind of logic is appropriate. One shouldn't expect much more of children at that age because they are generally incapable of abstracting any higher principles of morality.

Children with stage-one moral reasoning have no understanding of the practical purpose for rules of behavior, or the idea that rules allow a society to function by creating a foundation of stability and security. They know only that rules are imposed by people in power (the adults) to keep those younger and smaller in line or simply to boss them around. The "smart" person seems to be the one who figures out how to get around the rules without being caught, or to manipulate the rules to her advantage.

This is why stage-one children cannot internalize rules or conceptualize them as fundamental principles. Morality is perceived as a one-way street. Kids are controlled by adults, younger children by the older, the weaker by the stronger. There is no concept of "give and take," of relationships in which both parties get something of what they want. Stage one is an all-or-nothing level at which power is the only key to behavior.

Some older children, of course, as well as many adults, still function on this level. They suffer from what we might rightfully call "arrested moral development." Their moral growth did not keep pace with their physical development. It is just such children who can cause serious problems at home, in school, and in the world, for they have never internalized an understanding of morality that is based on principles of the common good.

When They Ask You "Why," Tell Them

One way to nurture your children's moral development at every stage is by giving them reasons for your desires, their rules, and the consequences for breaking the rules. The favorite response of most parents to the question "Why?" with respect to rules for behavior—"Because I say so"—is a morally limiting response. Studies indicate that the children of parents who base their demands for ethical behavior solely on their authority tend not to develop beyond this fear-of-punishment stage. The trick even at this level is to support your appropriate expressions of parental authority by helping your children work through the moral reasoning involved in your decisions

This may seem like a contradiction, but it isn't. Taking the time, care, and patience to explain moral reasoning is what good parents have been doing for generations, even with children who are developmentally too young to understand such reasoning. It is never too soon to begin teaching your children why it's important to treat others with kindness, to be trustworthy, not to steal. It is never too early to begin teaching them by word and example the relationship between behaving ethically and creating the kind of world we would all like to live in. Children will add to their understanding of this lesson with every stage of moral development they attain. Each stage will reveal another layer of insight about the "big picture" and will lead to the discoveries of the next.

🍃 Stage Two: An Eye for an Eye

After children have passed through the lowest stage of moral reasoning, they arrive at the level of payback—"An eye for an eye, and a tooth for a tooth." This is the principle of exacting damages in kind for injuries, real or imagined. If someone punches you in the arm, you feel compelled to punch him back. If someone steals your notebook, you steal hers in return. *Everything* has to be paid back—physical injury, verbal abuse, a mean face—or life is somehow out of balance. By the same reasoning, those who do something good for you must be paid back as well. At this stage of moral development, the ledger sheet must be kept in balance, for it is fairness that is the key.

"That's Not Fair!"

Children functioning on this second level seem to live lives of moral indignation. They believe that everything ought to be "fair," by which they usually mean "equal." If they get punished for breaking a certain rule, then so should everyone. If younger brother gets a present when it's not his birthday, fairness demands that older sister get one too. When this doesn't happen, outrage results, in the form of sulking, screaming, or tears. The child may even internalize the apparent disparity and feels that she is worth less as a person than her brother.

An important concept to teach them is that fair does not necessarily mean "equal" or "the same." It may rather mean giving a child what he or she needs. Everybody doesn't necessarily need the same thing at any given time. Big sister may need a new sweater, while little brother may need new shoes. This may seem reasonable to an adult, but either or both of the children may feel that you're not being "fair." It is necessary with children at this stage to continually point out the difference between fairness and equality. Demonstrate by your actions the idea that fairness simply means that each child is treated with respect in his or her own right, and that what is most important is that all people are treated with equal kindness, care, and dignity.

You can also point out to your children that life *isn't* always fair, despite our best intentions. When they come to you with a grievance about being treated unfairly, it's okay for you to say,

"You know, I agree with you. That really doesn't seem fair, does it? Sometimes things don't work out the way we think they should. What do you think we might do when that happens?" Engage them in a conversation about life's accidents and injustices. Share with them experiences in which you too were angry because things didn't work out "fairly." Tell them that even though things didn't work out fairly for them, they still have the opportunity to treat other people fairly, which is the way your children themselves would like to be treated. It's a tough lesson for young children to absorb, but talking about it may help them move on to higher levels of moral development.

Build Moral Reasoning

At this stage, however, what children mean by "fair" often means getting what they *want*. At this concrete, physical level, they understand right or wrong according their ability to touch and see the results of their behavior. They are generally not capable of understanding that fairness involves more than equal subjection to rules the adults have imposed; that it is based on broader principles of justice. You can't expect stage-two children to realize that if they lie or steal from someone, it undermines fairness. At this level, such concepts as trust and integrity have no meaning. It is only at the next stage that children can begin to appreciate the abstraction of a universal code of ethics as the basis of a "fair" society. Nevertheless, you can begin to guide them toward higher levels if you couple your example with a higher-level explanation of *why* you act the way you do.

For example: A neighbor accidentally leaves his sunglasses at your house. When you return them to their owner, take your child with you. On the way over, point out to the child (who may be reasoning on the level of "finders keepers") why it is important to return the sunglasses to Mr. Clay: because you wouldn't want to live in a community in which people kept other people's things. You might ask your child to imagine what the world would be like if you couldn't trust your neighbors to return lost things. This helps to stretch his ethical understanding from one stage of moral development up to the next.

Taking the time to build your children's moral reasoning has other benefits as well. It is an important way to demonstrate and model respect. Children, regardless of age, respond more fully and wholeheartedly when they are accorded respect and dignity. Your gift of time and attention enhances their self-esteem and places them one step nearer to developing the habit of granting others respect and dignity in return. As children develop their moral reasoning, they gradually leave the tightly controlled world of self-centeredness and self-gratification. Their emotional horizons expand to include the welfare and feelings of others and a realization of the interconnectedness of all human beings.

Take Time to Develop Your Relationship

In the end, your success at helping your children reach the next stage of moral development depends on your having developed a relationship with them based on love, trust, understanding, openness, and integrity. If you have consistently modeled these qualities for them, if you have consistently shown them that who they are and what they have to say is important, they are more likely to accept your guidance on moral reasoning. They are more likely to share their internal debates about ethical issues with you (rather than just doing what they want and sneaking around behind your back to avoid being caught) when they know that you are willing to listen to their point of view, to admit your mistakes, to compromise. They are more likely to move easily to the next stage of moral development when your parenting at this stage has guided them in seeing you, and all sources and symbols of authority, as something more than simply powers to be avoided and manipulated for their own ends.

Developing such relationships takes time. You cannot expect success if you wait until your children are nearing adolescence. You need to spend time nurturing a teaching relationship from their earliest years, through hundreds of simple joint activities and interactions. The specifics are not important. They may be as simple as taking a walk, having a picnic, visiting the library, or seeing a play or a basketball game. The important thing is to create opportunities for focused one-on-one time with each child.

Appeal to a Higher Moral Level

As you establish your credibility with your children, do what you can to help them move forward along the path of ethical development. Your goal is to encourage them to experience a sense of connection with other people of all ages, genders, nationalities, and races—to appreciate that their sorrows, joys, frustrations, and triumphs are of the same quality as their own.

To stretch your children's sense of empathy, you must consciously appeal to higher levels of moral reasoning than simple "fairness" or equal treatment. When you ask your children to do something for you or for another member of the family, you might appeal to *love* rather than reciprocity. "Do this because we're a family," or "because that's the way people should behave toward one another," or "because it's the right thing to do" speaks to a higher level of moral reasoning than "Do this for me because I did that for you." If Judeo-Christian religious values are important in your family, reinforce such simple, yet powerful lessons as "Love your neighbor as yourself," or "Do to others what you would have them do to you." (An appropriate secular expression of this message is, "How would *you* feel if…") Such an understanding of what is truly "fair" will help your child become ready to function at the next stage of moral development.

 ## Stage Three: The Moral Mirror of Others

One reality that you can help children and adolescents face is that their sense of personal value depends, in no small degree, on the judgments of others. Our notions of what is right and wrong about our behavior are based to a great extent on the reflections we observe in the faces, words, and other responses of those around us. This fact carries both positive and negative implications, which you can explain to your children.

On the positive side, your children will learn that one reason to be a good person is so that others will think highly of us, and we in turn will think well of ourselves. On the negative side, there is the danger of turning our ethical judgments over to others entirely, thereby abdicating personal responsibility for our actions and their consequences. As children at this stage inevitably seek the approval of their parents and peers (and, to some degree, their teachers), one of the greatest moral challenges they face is to allow the expectations of these outside forces into their developing value system without letting them dictate to their conscience.

This is yet another reason why raising ethical children is a complex, challenging experiment. It requires delicate balances between holding on and letting go, between control and freedom, between guidance and independence, between protecting children from negative influences and allowing them to explore the world on its own terms. Ideally, as your children grow toward maturity, they will establish a foundation of ethical behavior on which they will eventually build their own secure moral self-image. If your examples and lessons have helped them make this ethical identity strong enough, it will be able to stand on its own, regardless of the values and expectations of your children's peers.

Stage Four: Internalized Ethical Self-Image

In the normal course of growth and development, a child's ethical behavior is transformed from a "If this for you, what for me?" model of human interaction into an ethical self-image. At this stage, acting ethically—being a "good person"—is an expression of living up to an internalized standard that has come to represent the highest moral aspects of the child's self-concept.

When your children reach this stage, they have the capacity for moral empathy, for "walking a mile in the other person's moccasins." This allows them to introduce an element of ethical flexibility into their decision-making process. Now the world is seen less in terms of absolutes, black and white, good guys and bad guys, and more as a stage on which players struggle with their consciences to do the right thing despite their mistakes and poor choices. Justice begins to be tempered with mercy and compassion, and your children begin to appreciate the moral ambiguity inherent in so many of life's struggles and ethical choices.

Talk to Them About Moral Conflicts

Point out to your children examples of moral ambiguity and the internal ethical struggles of life. Think of situations in your personal relationships, the workplace, and school in which you had to make tough ethical decisions. Sharing these stories with your children and telling them how your choices ultimately affected you will better enable them to accept life's moral ambiguities. You can also use similar issues from the media. These everyday examples can serve as great discussion starters and help your children understand that no one can have moral certainty about every decision she makes. All we can do is make the best choices we can, based on the ethical principles we have learned.

Stage Five: Social Obligation

This stage takes young people beyond reasoning about their moral relationships to specific others to a more complex level where they begin to see themselves as part of a larger social system. Their internal questioning evolves from "What does it mean to be a good daughter [son, friend, etc.]?" to "What does it mean to be a moral member of my community [nation, religious group, etc.]?"

As young people explore what it means to be part of a social system, they discover that they are part of an interlocking network in which everyone must do his part to help the system function smoothly. For the first time in their lives, their personal responsibility projects onto the large screen of society. They experience the burden of obligation that comes with being a participating member of a social group.

It is only at this stage of moral reasoning that people are truly able to understand what "good citizenship" means. Only now can they appreciate the reasons for the intricate fabric of social rules on which a culture, consciously or not, must agree if it is to hold together. They come to realize that it isn't enough just to go along with what society has to offer. If people do not actively contribute something to the community, it will eventually retrogress to an amoral state of violence and apathy.

Here too, people begin to understand for the first time the true importance of self-respect. Their decisions are based on a desire to feel good about themselves, to demonstrate integrity in their behavior toward others, to be a person whose word can be trusted. They come to see these attributes as not merely desirable but necessary if others are to hold them in high esteem, and if they are to bring themselves closer to their own moral ideal.

Give Them an Ethical Reality Test

Young people at this stage are beginning to ask how their actions will affect others in their social system. They start to feel responsible for more than their own tiny sphere of influence. They are often torn between the powerful competing interests of peer pressure and the desire to stand on their own. They are easily influenced by the likes, dislikes, and cultural fashions of their social group, yet their search for self-identity encourages them to find a way to stand out from the crowd. Now when they contemplate the question, "What would the world be like if everyone acted just the way I do?" they consciously hope that the answer they receive is positive and encouraging.

Because of this emotional tug-of-war, it can be useful to share this "ethical reality projection" with children who have reached this stage of moral reasoning. "What would the world be like if everyone did what I am thinking about doing?" is a concrete, compelling, easily understood way of gauging ethical decisions. Adolescents can often see that being socially responsible means acting in such a way that *they* can serve as models of appropriate ethical behavior for others, just as they look to older, more experienced people as their own models.

Offer Simple Rules for Complex Choices

One way to help your children reach this stage of moral reasoning is to encourage them to develop a sense of independence and an ability to make decisions. Another is to take the time frequently to help them be aware of their place in the wider social context. Teach your children about the various levels of society in which we all fit: the family system, work or school, and social, spiritual and political communities. Encourage their participation in scouting, youth groups, team sports, community activities, and other social worlds that allow them to live their lives as members of diverse interlocking circles.

A third way of introducing your children to complex social systems is to point out the various alternatives that are possible in making ethical decisions. Show them examples of positive self-regard and demonstrations of self-respect: young women who say "no" to sexual pressure, adults and children who are willing to stand up for what they believe in defiance of an opposing majority. Pass along simple rules to live by. For example, when your child is faced with a behavioral decision involving another person, ask her, "Would it be okay if the situation were reversed?" If the answer is "yes," she can be fairly certain that the behavior she is contemplating is appropriate.

Another approach is a form of imaginary role-playing. Ask your child to imagine that he is the other person in a two-way disagreement, and to express and explain that person's point of view. When he argues the opposite point of view as though he were passionately committed to it, he may be surprised how easily he can develop a sense of empathy and understanding for it.

Yet another technique is to ask, "How would you feel if...?" Thinking about how they would feel if they were a substitute teacher dealing with a rude and disruptive student, for example, or a storeowner dealing with petty theft, will help get children out of their usual modes of thinking and force them to imagine another person's perspective. This experience helps broaden their ability to view any issue from several possible angles, and expands their understanding of the diversity of viewpoints among people whose life experiences are different from their own.

You can also achieve these goals by sharing with children stories about the world outside their community. Expose them to books, movies, and other media that will give them an appreciation for life beyond their sphere of experience and understanding. Talk about important, ethically challenging events that are happening in the world, and involve them in thinking about the ethical choices inherent in the social and political issues of the day.

Don't fall into the trap of wanting always to simplify life. We seem to prefer straightforward problems with "yes" or "no" answers, even though the truth usually lies somewhere in between. It isn't important to be able to give your children the "right" answers to complex moral questions. It is more important to engage them in the process of examining issues and realizing their complexity. The key is to help your children learn to live with life's ambiguities, to celebrate its complexity, and to feel okay about the apparent paradoxes in their own thinking.

Most important is how you *act* with regard to these complex social issues. Do your children see you becoming involved, giving your time and resources to causes in which you believe, and demonstrating a sense of personal responsibility toward society? If not, how can they be expected to develop a social conscience of their own? Never forget that you are their first and most influential role model. Always.

Stage Six: Spiritual Democracy and Personal Responsibility

The highest form of moral reasoning is the ability to look past the self and understand that society is based on universal principles that unite all people simply because they are human beings. The foundation for ethical behavior at this stage of moral development is the principle of respect for the inalienable rights of individuals: personal integrity and worthiness, freedom from oppression and abuse, the pursuit of one's dreams and goals in consistency with the general social good. These are rights that belong to everyone by reason of birth, that are contained in the very definition of a human being.

This idea expresses what I like to think of as "spiritual democracy." It implies that all persons deserve to be treated as moral equals. This level of moral reasoning lets us evaluate any political or social system on the basis of how well it respects, encourages, and nurtures these rights. It is only when an individual functions at this level that the concept of "civil disobedience" has any meaning, for it implies that one is held to a higher ethical standard than "keeping society running smoothly."

The Mahatma Gandhis and Martin Luther King, Jrs. of the world functioned at this moral level, but so do countless unknown people. Our goal is to help raise the level of moral discourse within our families and our communities so that our children naturally aspire to create a world that encourages, inspires, and empowers the individual to self-actualization and fulfillment.

This is the level of true democracy, of respect for cultural pluralism and diversity. It is this moral level to which our political system allegedly aspires and which our social system claims to champion. It is an appeal to a higher moral order. We want our children to envision this spiritually democratic society as a world that they can help create—a world that encourages every human being to fulfill his or her unique potential. To work toward this common vision is truly the highest good. To pass such a vision on to our children is truly within our power as parents.

The Complex Makeup of Human Beings

Don't make the mistake of thinking that this overview of the stages of moral development represents an absolute, step-by-step progression. Human beings are complicated beings. It is impossible to predict with one hundred percent accuracy how a person will act at any given time in any specific circumstance. When children move to higher levels of moral reasoning, they don't simply shed their previous moral understandings reptile fashion. Instead, they take their new understanding and new interpretations of what things mean and integrate them into their newly emerging realities.

All of us as parents want our children to fulfill themselves as individuals and to form caring, responsible relationships with others and with the world. It is our responsibility to help guide them down the right path. The rest is up to them.

How to Guide Your Children
Through the Stages of Moral Development

■ Recognize that children's moral reasoning develops
in stages, from a conception of rules based solely on
power through notions of equal treatment, awareness
of others' responses to their behavior, and moral sense
of self to a socially directed sense of ethics and
personal responsibility.

■ Do not expect your children to demonstrate an
understanding of morality beyond a level appropriate
to their development.

■ At the same time, build moral reasoning by teaching
your children rules of ethical behavior that are a step
beyond their current understanding.

*Leading Your Children
to Ethical Choices
in Everyday Life*

KEY #4

Demonstrate Unconditional Love

While I was working on this book, my six-year-old niece went to a pet store to buy a gerbil. The wise owner of the store told her, "First pick it up and hold it. If you can't cuddle with it, then you aren't ready to keep it as a pet."

This story made me wonder, "How come nobody ever asks the same of potential parents before they are allowed to take kids home?" Every child deserves affection, attention, positive reinforcement and unconditional love to develop a strong sense of self-worth. Only then will they see other human beings as worthy of their love and care—of being treated ethically.

Why We Should Love Them for Who They Are

Children need to know they are loved, unconditionally. Showing a child love and acceptance from her first year of life is the foundation of ethical action. Holding, touching, kissing, and otherwise demonstrating love for your children is the keystone that holds together all the other spiritual, emotional, and social building blocks.

Children need to know they are valuable. They need to know they are important enough for you to take time to be with them individually, to notice what they are doing, how they dress, what they have created, how they are growing. Such seemingly small things are more important to a child's sense of self than we can ever realize. As the philosopher and teacher Henry James wrote, "The deepest principle of human nature is the craving to be appreciated." When children receive consistent, appropriate demonstrations of acceptance and approval from their parents, they inevitably interpret them as signifying, "I am worthwhile, valuable, and lovable."

There is perhaps no greater lesson that our children can learn. Belief in themselves empowers them with the inner security they need to respect and love others in return. Loving attachment to a parent figure is the crucial first step toward building the positive self-image necessary for ethical behavior as an adult.

The test of unconditional love is the "unconditional" part. It means that our love for our children does not come and go depending on whether or not they remembered to do their chores or got into a fight at school. It means that we love them for who they are, not for how they act from moment to moment. It means that they are worthy of our love simply because they are our children— not because they are "good" or "obedient" children.

Separate Behavior from the Child

Unconditional love does *not* mean that you don't discipline your children or correct their negative behavior. It isn't what you do; it's how you do it. Strict rules clearly and consistently enforced can communicate love to children, if you consistently demonstrate with praise and physical affection that the love you bear them is not dependent on their behavior.

Demonstrating such love is not always easy. When we are upset or irritated, it is often difficult to distinguish between the child and his behavior. It's too easy for us to lash out with our parental-judgment reflex, inappropriately labeling him as bad, stupid, dumb, thoughtless, irresponsible, or untrustworthy.

To get across the point that we disapprove of the child's behavior while keeping intact the unconditional nature of our love, we must *focus on the behavior and not on the child.* It isn't who he is that upsets us; it's what he has done. This may seem like a small thing, perhaps too subtle to be meaningful, but it makes a big difference to our children when they hear us criticizing their *behavior* instead of condemning *them.*

"It's not okay to leave your baby brother unattended" preserves a child's emotional well-being far better than, "You wicked, irresponsible thing!" It conveys the message that we dislike what she has done, not who she is. "I don't like it when you grab the last cookie" makes your point far more effectively than "You're a greedy, selfish pig!" It criticizes the child's behavior without demeaning the essential nature of her being.

Demonstrate Love Daily

Keep in mind at all times the importance of demonstrating your unconditional love each day. Some people find it a useful technique to actually practice finding one or two occasions daily to show their unconditional love to each child.

This does not mean bringing home a present every day. It does mean bestowing such emotional gifts as hugs and kisses, verbal acknowledgment of your love, and positive reinforcement of the child's inherent value. In this way, parents form the habit of relating to their children from a position of unconditional love, and children get the emotional nourishment they so deeply need.

Benjamin West, one of the first Americans to win recognition as an artist, used to tell about a childhood incident in which he painted a portrait of his sister on the kitchen floor. When his mother came home, before directing him to clean up the mess, she looked at him and exclaimed, "What a beautiful picture you have made of your sister!" Then she bent down and kissed him. "With that kiss," West later recalled, "I became a painter."

Unconditional love is crucial to the emotional health of every child. It is essential if children are to feel valuable enough to extend the same love to others, thereby increasing rather than decreasing the store of compassion in the world. Only parents have the power to bestow this blessing. Without it, children are doomed to a life of inner conflict and pain. With it, there are no limits to what they can accomplish.

How to Show Your Children
that Your Love Is Unconditional

- Demonstrate unconditional love daily with hugging, kissing, and positive words.

- Base your love on who they are, not on what they do.

- Demonstrate acceptance and approval of your children every day.

- Take every opportunity to praise their positive behavior.

- Address your children's negative behavior while reinforcing that your love is not conditional on their behavior.

*Leading Your Children
to Ethical Choices
in Everyday Life*

KEY #5

Endow Your Children with Self-Esteem

Imagine that you had it in your power to give your children the one gift which, above all others, would most help them to create lives of success, purpose, meaning, satisfaction, and joy. One quality, characteristic, or possession—what would it be? According to nearly every contemporary child-development expert, that gift would be self-esteem.

Typical of the many studies on the causes and effects of self-esteem was one conducted by Dr. Stanley Coopersmith of the University of California (in *Raising Good Children*, by Thomas Lickona). He discovered that there were clearly identifiable differences between the family lives of children who exhibited high self-esteem and those who exhibited low self-esteem. Parents of high self-esteem kids generally demonstrated more love and acceptance of their children through simple everyday expressions of affection and attention than did the parents of low self-esteem kids. The latter parents tended to be highly critical and vocally judgmental of their children most of the time.

At the same time, contrary to what "conventional wisdom" might suggest, the parents of high self-esteem kids were less permissive, less ambiguous, and more consistent about their expectations for their children's behavior. The parents of low self-esteem kids tended to be inconsistent and unclear about their expectations. Either they never set rules, or they didn't follow through with enforcement of their rules.

In addition, children with high self-esteem tended to come from families with an overall democratic tone and practice. They grew up believing that their opinions mattered, even when they were quite young. Their parents paid attention to them and to their needs and wants, and took their suggestions and contributions seriously.

What are the differences between a child with high self-esteem and a child with low self-esteem? You can reasonably measure your children's behavior and attitudes against these standards with the **"Self-Esteem Checklist on pages 92–93.**

Self-Esteem Checklist

To gain an approximate assessment of the level of your child's self-esteem, check off the items that describe him or her.

A child with high self-esteem:

☐ Is proud of his or her accomplishments.

☐ Can act independently.

☐ Assumes responsibility.

☐ Can tolerate frustration.

☐ Approaches challenges with enthusiasm.

☐ Feels capable of taking charge of situations in his or her own life.

☐ Has a good sense of humor.

☐ Has a sense of purpose.

☐ Can postpone gratification.

☐ Seeks help when needed.

☐ Is confident and resourceful.

☐ Is active and energetic, and spontaneously expresses his or her feelings.

☐ Is relaxed and can manage stress.

A child with low self-esteem:

☐ Avoids situations that require risk-taking.

☐ Feels powerless.

☐ Becomes easily frustrated.

☐ Is overly sensitive.

☐ Always needs reassurance.

☐ Is easily influenced by others.

☐ Frequently uses the phrases "I don't know," and "I don't care."

☐ Is withdrawn.

☐ Blames others for his or her failures.

☐ Is isolated, has few friends, is preoccupied.

☐ Is uncooperative and angry.

☐ Is uncommunicative.

☐ Is clingy and dependent.

☐ Is constantly complaining.

☐ Has a generally negative attitude.

Adapted from *Self-Esteem: The Key to Your Child's Well-Being*, by H. Clemes and R. Bean.

How We Affect Our Children's Self-Esteem

Everyone uses other people as "mirrors" to reflect their personal social stature. To some degree, we all judge our self-worth on a scale created by others. Children observe how they are treated by peers, then use this external scale as a gauge to determine their level of "popularity." Similarly, they watch their teachers for clues to whether they are "smart" or dumb."

But children's most important mirrors by far are their parents. How we treat our children, the tone of voice in which we address them, the degree of respect with which we respond to their ideas, opinions, or contributions to conversation, all have a powerful effect on their sense of personal worth.

Simply put, positive self-images produce positive, socially acceptable behavior, while negative self-images produce negative, unacceptable behavior. One way or another, we unconsciously modify our behavior to match our inner expectations. Children who act out in negative ways are often found to be doing so primarily to match their behavior to a pre-formed poor self-image.

This is a classic example of a self-fulfilling prophecy. We want to be consistent with our self-image, and so we act in ways that will make us feel more secure—by tuning our behavior to how we think someone "like us" is supposed to act in a given situation. After all, everyone wants to be right (especially when it comes to ourselves), so we will behave in such a way that will prove ourselves right.

The good news, however, is that the self-fulfilling prophecy works both ways. Children who think they are good, capable, lovable, and competent will act so as to demonstrate that they do indeed possess these qualities. This is why it is so important to instill a sense of positive expectations in each of our children.

The task of helping to build our children's self-esteem is crucial, not only for their ethical development but for success and satisfaction in every aspect of their lives. Fortunately, we have a number of tools available to help us meet this challenge.

Celebrating Your Children's Uniqueness

One of our primary tools for helping our children develop self-esteem is the miracle of any child's uniqueness. We must help our children understand how miraculous it is that there is only one of them among all the world's billions of people. No one else on earth, no matter how smart, beautiful, strong, talented, or rich, can ever be a better version of themselves than they can be. *They* will always be the best at being themselves, and their true challenge in life is to make that unique self the best it can be.

This understanding is important because our sense of who we are is under constant scrutiny throughout our lives. Parents and teachers, siblings and peers, co-workers and bosses, romantic partners and spouses all too often lead us to feel that there are external, objective, universal standards against which we are being measured—standards of behavior, standards of competence, standards of social skills, and physical attractiveness. Such a constant sense of being compared with a (mythical) ideal can lead us to feel inferior, less than adequate to the task of successfully negotiating life's challenges. This sense can wreak havoc with children's sense of self-worth. This is why it is crucial to drum into their consciousness the reality of their uniqueness until it becomes part of the fabric of their being.

Think of it in the biological sense. Every baby that is conceived starts out from the moment of fertilization as a winner of a lottery against hugely greater odds than any wager in the history of gambling. An individual egg and an individual sperm joined together to form a once-only-for-all-time combination.

The same holds true in the spiritual sense. The realization of uniqueness can be one of the most empowering discoveries of a child's life. Imagine how free he will feel when he truly understands that the only person worth comparing himself to is—himself! When our children recognize themselves to be the special, extraordinary creations that they are, it can't help but increase their store of self-esteem.

How to Use the Power of Your Words

In her marvelous book, *The Magic of Encouragement,* Stephanie Marston describes the power that parents' words have on their children's developing sense of self-worth. She cites a study by Jack Canfield, when he was at the University of Iowa, in which graduate students spent a day following average two-year-olds from average families. They discovered that these toddlers received a total of 432 negative messages from their parents (such as "Don't touch that!" or "You're not big enough to do that!") as compared with 32 positive messages. At this rate, is it any wonder that kids grow up feeling insecure about their abilities, feeling inadequate to negotiate the ups and downs they encounter in the world, perhaps even feeling less than worthwhile and lovable?

Ms. Marston points out the obvious but important parenting behaviors that enhance children's self-esteem, such as focusing on the behavior and not the child, and taking the time to build on a child's strengths. Obviously, parents need to establish clear consequences for their children's negative behavior, and we'll be taking a look at how to do this in a later chapter. For now, it's important to recognize that such behaviors as stealing, lying, and bullying are the natural result of children feeling negative about themselves. Parents need to understand and address the root causes of the negative feeling as well as the behavior. It is often easier and more effective, in fact, to remove the cause of your child's expression of anger or frustration than to impose punishment in response to it.

Develop the Habit of Praise

Without question, the most successful parents are those who have their eyes and ears open to their children's doing things well. Any child is better served when his parents are as vigilant at picking out the correct answers in his homework paper as they are about spotting the mistakes. Any parent is more successful if she acknowledges the times her child *does* clean her room or dress neatly as often as she points out when the room needs cleaning or when the child wears jeans with holes in the knee (which of course in any given year could be a key middle-school fashion statement).

Developing the habit of noting and acknowledging your child's positive attributes can be one of the most liberating experiences of your parenting career. Very few things are more satisfying to children or provide a greater sense of self-worth than having their parents acknowledge the things they do well. As children become increasingly exposed to the world's complexity, as they come to feel more like tiny plankton in a vast sea and less like individuals who matter to anyone, simple attention and validation by their parents takes on all the more significance and power.

All you have to do to understand the power of a parent's approval or disapproval is to think about your relationship with your own parents. Our desire for parental approval continues to affect our feelings about ourselves no matter how old we get, no matter whether our parents are living or dead.

Living things need sunshine to grow and flourish. Praise, acknowledgment, and encouragement are the simple yet powerful ways we bring sunshine into our children's lives. Every negative comment is like a spate of rain that washes a bit of self-esteem away. We all know people who seem to go through life with their own personal thunderstorm hovering over their heads. This attitude can be largely attributed to their having internalized parental disapproval of their behavior to the degree that they have come to believe they are inherently bad, even failures in life.

When you think about it, it isn't so surprising that parents dwell on their children's negative behavior. After we teach them what behavior is expected of them, we tend to expect them to do the right thing every time: "If I tell her to do something, she should simply do it. Why should I have to reward her for it?"

We tend to think this way because we forget that proper social behaviors are skills that our children are *learning*. Like any skills, they are learned only through repeated practice. Since we assume proper behavior, we jump on our kids every time they deviate from our expectation. Good behavior goes unacknowledged because it doesn't seem worthy of special notice.

It is important to see your children as students of behavior, with you as their teacher. Just as you wouldn't expect them to master a foreign language without repeated practice, so too it should be with positive social behavior. If you look on each action you approve of as a symbol of progress, you will find it easier to acknowledge that action with a positive comment. Remember, the more you reinforce children's positive behavior, the more effectively they will learn it.

One of my favorite stories illustrating this point happened in a preschool classroom. There was a little boy named Adam who wasn't particularly outstanding at anything. One day when his mother came to pick him up, he had a large gold star pinned to his shirt. Thrilled and amazed, his mother hugged him and asked, "Adam, what did you do to earn that wonderful gold star?"

Adam, puffed up with the pride of his accomplishment, replied, "Well, every day we rest, and today *I* rested the best!"

Now, here was a brilliant teacher. She found something that the child was doing right, and she rewarded him for it. There is no surer way to build a child's self-esteem.

You are your children's number-one teacher. Find reasons to praise them every day. Make a point of it—give yourself a daily "homework" assignment of rewarding each child with two positive statements. Try it for three weeks. I promise that you will see positive, even dramatic results in your children and in yourself.

Help Your Children Experience Competence

Like Adam, all children need experiences of competence both large and small that demonstrate to themselves that they can accomplish tasks entrusted to them and can be counted on to meet challenges successfully. This is why it is important to give them small tasks to do around the house, beginning at an early age. It doesn't much matter what the responsibility is, as long as it is something that the child can accomplish, so that his experience is one of self-satisfaction and success.

In this way, one step at a time, children progress into accepting greater responsibility. Success builds on success, until the child believes unassailably that he can accomplish just about anything he chooses to attempt. This is truly a mark of self-esteem and a key element of success—the openness to take on new challenges without being paralyzed by the fear of failure.

Find Little Ways to Show You Believe in Them

If you look back on your life, you will probably acknowledge that it was the little things, the small gestures of support, encouragement, and love, that meant the most to you. Whether they came from a parent, a work colleague, a high-school sweetheart or a life companion, these simple, heartfelt reminders of their faith in you meant more than all the rewards of a lifetime.

One of my fondest childhood memories is of lunchtime in the school cafeteria. I assure you, it wasn't due to the quality of the food! Rather, it was because every time I brought my lunch to school, I would open the bag to discover that my mother had included a personal note with the lunch. Inevitably the note would tell me that she loved me, believed in my ability to succeed, and knew I would make it a successful day.

Few feelings in life are more wonderful than the inner glow that comes from knowing your parents are on your side, believe in you, and will stand by you through thick and thin. So, my next suggestion is to do what my mother did: When you send your child off to school, slip an encouraging note in with her lunch. Find other occasions for positive notes too. You can never acknowledge your children too much. You can never remind them too often that they are lovable, capable, and worthy of your confidence.

Filling the Cup of Self-Esteem Every Day

As a parent, you have the opportunity every day to give your children gifts of the heart. They are simple, they take very little time, and yet they can have a powerful impact on children's self-esteem that can last them all their lives.

One of the easiest ways to keep track of how well you are reinforcing your children's feelings of self esteem is to ask yourself these questions every evening: "If it were entirely a result of what I said and did today, how would my children feel about themselves as human beings? What have I done today to fill their cup of self-esteem to overflowing?" As you honestly answer these questions, you will provide yourself with a built-in guide for establishing the parenting style and relationship with your children that sets them on the path to becoming ethical adults.

I believe that parenting is the task of leading our children on a unique treasure hunt, where they themselves are the treasure. It is an adventure in self-discovery that requires us, their parents, to serve as guides, cheerleaders, sources of inspiration, and models of behavior. By fulfilling this role, we empower our children to see themselves as capable of success in this lifelong challenge of self-discovery.

How to Nurture Self-Esteem in Your Children

- Recognize that self-esteem is the most important factor in creating lives of purpose, meaning, and success.

- Have clear, consistent expectations of your children's behavior.

- Honor your children's opinions and suggestions.

- Help your children appreciate their uniqueness.

- Give your children opportunities to develop and demonstrate their competence.

*Leading Your Children
to Ethical Choices
in Everyday Life*

KEY # 6

Empower Your Children with Consequences for Behavior

One of the great challenges of ethical parenthood is learning to love our children even when they are acting rudely, rebelliously, or obnoxiously. All children consider it their duty to test the limits of their acceptable behavior and our tolerance. As parents, we are ethically responsible for setting and maintaining these limits. We are obligated to establish the moral climate in our home and to define the kinds of behavior we will not tolerate.

We know that children respond positively to parents who empathize with their struggles, emotional traumas, and difficult decisions. But when parents allow a child to get away with unacceptable behavior, they are doing serious moral damage to the child. This is because a significant part of a child's sense of security comes from having parents they can depend on for moral strength, guidance, and correction—in a word, for discipline.

Discipline, simply put, is teaching a child the way he or she should act. It is training, positive reinforcement of desired behavior, rewards to encourage positive self-esteem, and demonstrations of correct social and ethical behavioral expectations. Discipline involves everything you do to help your children learn to be the kind of person you want them to become.

Modeling Self-Control

Like your values, your discipline style teaches by example. It demonstrates standards that your child will inevitably emulate. You want your child to become a fulfilled, ethical adult who is engaged in a lifelong process of learning and self-actualization. It follows that to achieve this goal, you must model correct social and ethical behavior, positively reinforce such behavior in your children, and follow an approach to rules and limits that preserves a child's sense of self-esteem. As Dr. Howard Hendricks puts it in *Family Happiness Is Homemade,* the secret of having a disciplined child is to be a disciplined parent.

Many parents wonder how they can maintain this standard when children act out in negative ways or otherwise challenge their rules and limits. The worst thing parents can do when this happens is, unfortunately, something they tell me they do all too often: "I know I shouldn't act this way with my child, but I just keep losing it. I hold things in and bottle up my feelings until they explode out of control and make an emotional mess all over the place. I lose sight of the impact I have. I wish I had some clear guidelines to follow so that parenting wouldn't stress me out so much!"

That, exactly, is what this key is about—how to engage in that automatic, daily role modeling that demonstrates the behavior you desire and allows you to make the kind of parenting choices that you can look back on with satisfaction and approval.

Why You Should Be a Parent, Not a Pal

Too frequently, it seems, parents act as though they aren't sure what their role is. Of course we want to have open, trusting relationships with our children, but this should not mean giving up our authority and treating our children as peers. Why should children respect the demands of a peer? Your job is not to be your children's pal; it is to give them guidance, support, caring, moral direction, and unconditional love. *You don't want to befriend your children*—not until they grow into adults.

The wonderful truth is, when you teach your children discipline, you give them an important tool for future success and happiness. Proper, loving discipline gives children a strong sense of self and well-being and allows them to function on a high level in society. It is only through the development of inner discipline that we are empowered to set appropriate goals and to follow through to their achievement. It is only through discipline that we can create anything of beauty or value, whether it is a work of art, a functioning business, a piece of furniture—or a child.

Children *need* discipline. Study after study confirms that parents who run a "tight ship" with comprehensive, well-defined, value-based rules consistently enforced tend to raise children who value themselves highly, develop their own sense of ethics, and have greater respect and affection for their parents. When parents don't assume this responsibility, children may infer indifference. A lack of clearly expressed values and guidelines tends to create anxiety in children while at the same time reducing their ability to develop strong inner controls over their behavior.

Children *want* discipline. Some years ago, a Gallup poll indicated that graduating high-school seniors wished their parents had loved them enough to require more of them. The students knew that this was their parents' appropriate role and responsibility. They understood that clear expectations and guidelines were what they needed to grow into emotionally mature, functioning adults.

This is why creating an atmosphere of consistent, reliable discipline is so important. Through clear guidelines and expectations of moral behavior, and by demonstrating in your daily life that you believe such guidelines are important, you provide your children with the keys to competence.

Understanding the Distinction Between Punishment and Consequences

Ethical children have a strongly developed sense that what they do is important to their parents. Children must expect that when they behave inappropriately, in public or private, their parents will correct them according to established rules and guidelines.

At the same time, however, we have seen how crucial it is to respond to our children's positive, appropriate behavior with attention at least equal to that which we give their negative behavior. If we only notice them when they are "bad," they learn that being bad is the way to get our attention. It may be uncomfortable for a child to be yelled at by one's parents, but it is infinitely more desirable than being ignored.

You can't overacknowledge your children. They need your approval as much as they need the air they breathe or the food they eat. Acknowledging appropriate behavior on an everyday basis is one of the most vital elements in the parenting process. This is why I believe that the best approach to discipline is one based on consequences, not punishment.

Punishment Is Always Negative

Dr. Don Dinkmeyer, in an article titled "Teaching Responsibility: Developing Personal Accountability Through Natural and Logical Consequences," wrote the following explanation of the value of consequences over punishment as a basis for discipline:

> A child learns from consequences when his parents allow him to experience the results of his actions. Just as adults who have experienced the inconvenience of running out of gas are most apt to fill their tanks when the marker nears empty, the child who has experienced hunger because he forgot his lunch is more likely to remember to take the lunch bag from the refrigerator before leaving for school.

An eight-year-old child named Carin expressed the distinction this way: "A punishment is something a parent does to you. A consequence is something you do to yourself." **"The Difference Between Punishment and Consequences" chart on page 109** provides further explanation.

There is no such thing as a positive punishment. There *can* be positive consequences. With a consequence-based approach to discipline, you determine rules for your children's behavior that are based on your values. You determine and enforce a specific set of negative consequences for breaking the rules—and you also specify a set of positive consequences for appropriate behavior.

The Difference Between Punishment and Consequences

- Punishment reinforces power and authority.

- Punishment is personalized, implying a negative moral judgment that may or may not be true.

- Punishment is primarily concerned with past behavior.

- Punishment communicates disapproval, even disrespect.

- Punishment can be arbitrary.

- Punishment implies an authoritarian demand for obedience.

- Consequences reinforce natural order.

- Consequences distinguish between the action and the doer and are experienced as impersonal.

- Consequences focus on present and future behavior.

- Consequences can take place in a supportive, even friendly environment.

- Consequences are predictable and usually inevitable.

- Consequences reflect the important element of choice.

Consequences Give Children the Power of Choice

The key to the this approach is the issue of choice. It is the acknowledgment of the child's individual free will, exercised by her own mind and judgment. It empowers the child to feel that she can ultimately gain mastery over her environment. Without the power to make independent, thoughtful decisions that carry specific consequences, our children feel that they have no such control. They are robbed of the possibility to make personal choices that strengthen their sense of competence and self-esteem.

Punishment often gets in the way of discipline because it distracts both parent and child from the real issue—that we each must learn to live with the results of our own actions. When I asked eight-year-old Carin why she thought that giving consequences was better than punishing as a way for her parents to teach her discipline, she didn't say the obvious thing, that no child likes to be punished. Instead, she expressed her wise understanding that by letting the consequences of her actions provide the lesson, her parents let her experience personal responsibility. Without any prompting from me, she said that it is much better for parents to let their children see what happens when they act wrongly without jumping in with punishments that confuse the issue.

When instead of punishing your child you let him experience the consequences of his actions, you also demonstrate respect. You communicate that you trust him to learn and grow from his unfolding experience with choices, actions, and mistakes. Giving children the opportunity to make mistakes and to live with their results teaches them not only that their actions have consequences but also that their world will not collapse as a result of their poor or unlucky decisions.

How to Implement Consequence-Based Discipline: Your Behavior Reinforcement Guide

Our parenting decisions are too often made by the seat of our pants (and sometimes by the seat of *their* pants). It should come as a relief to know that here is an area in which we can actually plan and prepare. On the sample **"Consequence-Based Discipline Plan"** below, take a look at how you might set up a simple system of positive and negative consequences based on one of your core values—responsibility, for example.

SAMPLE PLAN

Consequence-Based Discipline Plan for Responsible Behavior

1. First, identify the specific examples of responsible behavior that you want to reinforce, *e.g.:* clearing the table, taking out the garbage, feeding the cat before school, finishing homework by 8:00 P.M. (It's best to limit the number of specific behaviors you're trying to reinforce at any given time, and to make them appropriate to your child's age.)

2. Establish specific positive consequences for appropriately following through with these responsibilities, *e.g.:* being allowed to watch an extra half-hour of television that day.

3. Establish specific negative consequences for noncompliance with the expected behaviors, *e.g.:* no computer games for three days.

The same principle can be followed for each of your core values. To reinforce perseverance, for example, you could create positive consequences for such behaviors as mowing the entire lawn, completing a long homework assignment, or writing thank-you notes for birthday gifts. You could set up negative consequences for failing to act in ways that demonstrate perseverance, as long as the tasks are reasonable for your child to complete.

Make a list of the positive behaviors you want to reward and a list of the negative acts you want to discourage. This gives you a handy "Behavior Reinforcement Guide" that you can refer to every day to keep your parenting on the right path. With this guide in hand, you can more easily base your decisions on previously made, conscious choices that you believe will move your children toward ethical behavior. Make sure your expectations are clear by discussing the expected behaviors and their consequences with your child and posting them in a prominent place.

What Positive Consequences Are Appropriate?

What are the most effective positive consequences we can give our children? This is a matter of continuing discussion and debate, and there is little absolute agreement among experts. Some maintain that we should never actually reward a child (as with money or toys) for positive behavior; that praise should be the only reinforcement. Others feel that for a reward to effectively reinforce positive behavior, it must be something that the child truly wants— whether a happy-face sticker, fifty cents, a small toy, a candy bar, or a hug. Still others say that it makes sense to tailor the consequences to the behavior (if you clear the table, you may decorate it for the next meal; when you finish writing your thank-you notes, you may have a stationery-creating art project). My own philosophy here, as with other aspects of parenting, can be summed up by what we may call *Reuben's Rule*: It goes like this: "Whatever works, works."

I believe it doesn't much matter what the specific reward is. What is effective for one parent and/or one child may not work for another. Either way, the principle is the same—the more ways you can invent to reward desired behavior, the more likely it is that your children will internalize that behavior. If it works for you and isn't harmful to your children, by all means give it a try.

The truth is, children often perceive their parents' behavior as a response to their actions. Whether intentioned or not, the ways you respond to a child's positive behavior—your smile, positive attention, language, and tone—will all reinforce her behavior. Since in effect you are already rewarding her, it is preferable to make such rewards part of a conscious plan rather than a chance happening. Find out what works as positive reinforcement for your child, and create a system that allows her to earn that reinforcement through her behavior.

Be Prepared with Consequences for Negative Behavior

Even with the most motivational positive reinforcements, there will be times when our children won't do what we want them to do. That's why we must have a system of negative consequences in place for those moments when they openly defy our wishes or act out in any of the infinite inappropriate ways that the active, creative minds of children can conceive. Hitting the neighbor's child in the face with a book, drawing on the dining-room table with a Magic Marker, and letting water in the sink run until it floods the bathroom floor only begin to suggest the possibilities.

Identify in writing the behavior that is unacceptable. Don't waste your time trying to create a fully comprehensive list; kids will always come up with new, improved crazy-making concepts. You may even ask your child's help in drawing up the list. Children can be very good (and often much harder on themselves than you would be) at coming up with their own personally appropriate list of thou-shalt-nots.

Now attach a negative consequence to each unacceptable behavior—taking away food treats or privileges, reducing TV time, or curtailing favorite activities are a few possible examples. The specifics will vary from home to home and from child to child. The trick is to discover those things that the child will perceive as negative. Being sent to one's room, for example, may be a negative consequence for some children but a positive reward for others. Again, if it seems reasonable to fit the consequence to the behavior (if you hurt the dog, you may not play with it for one day), by all means do it.

Be Consistent

One of the most difficult challenges caring parents face when it comes to effective discipline is the need to be consistent in their responses to their children's behavior. Consistency on the part of parents is vital because it leads to internal stability in children. Few things create greater insecurity in children than not knowing how their parents are going to react to what they do. When you discipline a child for "talking back" on one occasion and ignore the same behavior on another, the child cannot get a clear message about the inappropriateness of the behavior.

This is one of the values of consequence-based discipline. Being consistent with your responses to your children's behavior, both positive and negative, teaches them in a direct, concrete way that there are things in their world that they can count on. Because consistency communicates stability and security, it helps give them the emotional strength to approach and seek future experiences with eagerness, openness and curiosity.

Ralph Waldo Emerson was right when he said, "A foolish consistency is the hobgoblin of little minds." There well may be something foolish in consistency for its own sake, without regard for the appropriateness of your response to a given situation. Mitigating circumstances may sometimes dictate a different response. Everything you do must be tempered with reason and balance. As long as you are making conscious choices about discipline and the messages you are sending to your children, you need not worry about occasional departures from consistency.

Parents must maintain consistency as a team. Any conflict between partners with regard to their children's expected behavior or consequences for specific behaviors must be resolved through negotiation, as I outlined in the case of setting ethical parenting goals in Key #1. This applies even when parents are divorced and remarried, assuming the child shares time with both households. Only by feeling secure in knowing what to expect from their external environment will children develop the "internal behavior regulator" they will need to succeed as ethical adults.

Parenting: An Art, Not a Science

Before we leave the subject of discipline, I need to emphasize one more key point: You never know for sure how things are going to turn out. You never can tell whether an intended lesson about the consequences of behavior is going to materialize as you expect.

Certainly, parenting involves skills that can be learned, practiced, and strengthened. The process of guiding your children toward responsibility, emotional health, and ethical behavior can be deepened and refined. But there is always the element of surprise to be contended with—the element of the unknown that can catch you off guard, with delight as often as with frustration. It can remind you repeatedly that children are complex, remarkably unpredictable human beings. True, they can sometimes turn your best intentions into parenting disasters, but they are just as likely to turn disasters into remarkable successes.

Discipline must be understood as a learning opportunity for both parent and child. Rules and consequences, consistency and exceptions are issues that will be modified as your children change from year to year—sometimes from day to day! There are no magic formulas that will answer every question, address every issue, or respond to every situation that may arise. Learning to relax, be flexible and not become overly stressed about your child-rearing decisions will go a long way toward helping you make the correct decisions. The more you are open to a lifelong process of experimentation, the more successful you will be.

This is an approach that I strongly recommend. Not every suggestion in this book will match the specific needs of every parent or child. A cookbook approach to raising children of character, with recipes to answer every challenge, simply doesn't exist. The process involves too much trial and error.

That being understood, refer to the **"Parenting Skill-Builder" techniques on pages 117–118** for a couple of approaches that can help you develop skills to bring you closer to your goal.

 ## Doing the Best You Can

The role of discipline in raising ethical children is to create a home environment in which your children understand the behavior expected of them with regard to themselves and to others. In such an environment you guide them as consistently as is reasonable toward fulfillment of these expectations. The goals of this process are to nurture a sense of self-mastery in your children, to empower them to make the difficult, sometimes painful decisions that all human beings face in their daily lives, and to let them know that they can live with the consequences of their actions no matter how disagreeable they might be.

All you can do is the best you can. The principles for guiding your children toward disciplined, ethical behavior are easy to understand, but it can be hard for even the most effective parents to follow through with them consistently day after day. Appreciate your successes, and don't be too hard on yourself for your frustrations. Treat yourself with care and kindness, and know that if you are doing your best to create a caring and supportive yet firm and consistent ethical climate in your home, your children will most likely turn out just fine.

Parenting Skill-Builder

Create a Success Journal

Ideally, you want to live life every day as a model for your children. Of course, nothing in family life happens as smoothly and cleanly as that. Every family, every child, every parent, has good days and bad, moments when everything seems to be going beautifully and moments of emotional overload.

One technique parents find helpful for getting through the rough times is to keep a "Success Journal" in which they record the stories of their successful parenting experiences. You can use a ringed binder, pad of paper, notebook, or computer, whatever is convenient. It doesn't matter how short or long your entries are. Write about every occasion on which you feel good about your parenting choices, have a positive interaction with your child, or feel that she has learned a lesson about ethical behavior. Don't neglect those sweet, simple moments, such as a morning when everything went smoothly, or a bedtime experience that was warm, positive, and loving for you and your child.

Now, whenever a negative experience threatens your parental self-esteem, you can take out your Success Journal and revisit your triumphs. Review your journal, collect your thoughts, and remind yourself of the parent you wish to be. Recall the image you want to project to your children. Then restore yourself emotionally and take the steps necessary to be that parent.

It isn't easy to stay calm when your children are not responding to your discipline efforts. Sometimes they actually seem to go out of their way to defy you. These are the times to take out your journal and remind yourself of your past successes. You'll reaffirm that you do indeed have good parenting skills, and that you will be as successful with them in the future as you have been in the past.

Parenting Skill-Builder
Call on Your Outside Expert

This technique involves a bit of creative imagination. Imagine that you have an invisible parenting expert on call 24 hours a day, 365 days a year. This expert will appear on demand whenever you need to short-circuit a parenting crisis. He will give you advice, point out the negative consequences of what you are doing, or remind you of skills that you possess but may have lost sight of in your present emotional state.

Whenever you find yourself losing perspective (or control), call upon your Outside Expert. You can give the person a name if it makes her more concrete and easier to visualize. Some people find it helpful to imagine a real expert, such as Dear Abby, Dr. Joyce Brothers, or Dr. Benjamin Spock (or even Dr. Reuben). As you take slow, deep breaths, imagine the advice your expert would give you. Let your magical consultant help you step out of your narrowly focused emotional state and see the interaction with your child from a more objective, impersonal viewpoint.

In most cases, you already know an appropriate way of dealing with the situation; you've just let your emotions interfere with your judgment. That is why calling upon the Outside Expert of your choice works so well. It allows your own best sense and inner guide to reemerge from behind the wall of anger and frustration.

In fact, an effective method for reminding you that you already have the skills you need is to imagine that someone else has come to *you* for advice on how to interact with his children. What would you tell him? My experience is that in nearly every case, you will be giving yourself the best answer as well.

How to Implement
Consequences-Based Discipline

- Recognize that discipline is the establishment of a moral climate in your home and is not the same as punishment.

- Show your children by your example what it means to be a disciplined person.

- Consistently enforce rules and limits to guide your children in achieving your behavioral goals.

- Strengthen your children's self-esteem and sense of competence by giving them the power to make personal behavior choices.

- Let your children's behavior choices, positive or negative, carry specific consequences.

- Choose consequences for positive and negative behavior based on what you think will motivate your children.

- Be consistent in your responses to your children's behavior, but temper consistency with reason and balance.

- Don't expect perfection; don't become discouraged by occasional setbacks or loss of control.

*Leading Your Children
to Ethical Choices
in Everyday Life*

KEY #7

Look For "Teachable Moments"

One reason we need always to act in ways we would feel proud to have our children emulate is that we never know which of the countless moments we spend with our children will turn out to be those memorable, "teachable moments."

Sometimes we can't even identify these moments when they're happening. Think again of those invaluable moral lessons you learned from your parents' example. Chances are they were not lessons your parents consciously taught you but were insights you gained in casual moments your parents wouldn't even remember!

Much as we'd like to, we can't just schedule quality time to discuss morality. We can't simply write, "Teach Susan how to be an ethical person" in our daily calendar for 3:00 P.M. Sunday. Our children's real lessons come from being, living, and interacting with us in a hundred different ways we could never predict.

This is why an important key to teaching children ethical behavior is learning to recognize "teachable moments," through which your children can develop the habit of being aware of ethical challenges. This habit will put them a step up on those people who go through life without noticing the moral choices and dilemmas inherent in their everyday activities.

Of course, part of the frustration of parenting is that ultimately what we and our children learn from a given situation may be very different things, and often the actual learning that takes place is beyond our control. An encounter with a homeless woman on the street, for example, may strike you as a potential lesson about charity, while your child sees it as an issue of personal responsibility and choice. All we can do is to use the opportunities that present themselves every day to teach something of meaning and value to our children.

How to Turn Ordinary Moments into Teachable Moments

Any moment may be a teachable moment. A conflict within the family, an anecdote about something that happened in school, a newspaper story or a chance observation of an occurrence in the street can be seized upon as an opportunity for a lesson in ethics.

Two of my favorite examples come from that popular theater of ethics known as "television." I watched a lot of news coverage of the Los Angeles civil disturbances in 1992, and the single most powerful image for me (in fact, it was the incident that started me thinking about writing this book) was of mothers walking hand-in-hand with their children to loot stores. My first thought on seeing that image was *what were those children learning?* The situation must have been a moment of profound emotional intensity for them, a condition under which the deepest learning often takes place. But as I thought about it further, I asked myself what message my own child would have received if she had been watching with me. What would have been her response to the moral challenge inherent in that scene?

Example number two came in the aftermath of the Southern California earthquake of January, 1994. A news team was in the parking lot of a supermarket in an area that had been hit hard by the quake. People were panic-buying, laying in supplies against the possibility of a long-term disruption of services. Electric power was out, and store personnel were in the parking lot with flashlights, leading people into the store to buy things and leading them out again. As the camera recorded this scene, a store employee wheeled out one of those tall rolling carts filled with trays of meat. What happened then was like a cartoon. Everybody broke out of their orderly line and swept over the cart with a big swooshing sound. In seconds, everything was gone from the trays.

Then came the teachable moment: half the people grabbed the meat and ran. They literally ran away. The other half took some meat and got back in line to wait to be led into the store to pay for it, along with whatever else they were buying.

Be a Moral Moderator

When you experience scenes such as these with your children, either on television or in person, your role is to verbalize the implied ethical issues as you see them, whether as questions to your children or as a conversation with another adult: "What is that woman doing? Why is she stealing those things from the store? What do you think her child is learning? How would you feel if you were that child? What would it be like to walk down a street where everyone was doing that? How do you think the owner of the store would feel watching this on TV? How do you think the owner's kids would feel if they had to do without food, or clothes, or toys because their parents' store was looted? What do you think they and this woman's child might say to each other?"

And likewise: "What just happened in that parking lot? What would you do if you were there? Would you take the meat and run? What do think is the right thing to do in this situation? How do you think those people waiting in line felt about those who ran? What do you think the people who ran would say to them? How do you think that store worker feels about what is happening?"

It is important when having these discussions to suggest alternative ways that people might respond to the ethical dilemma, and to discuss them with your children. Thus your children will consistently see that there are always choices of behavior. It is in the quality of our choices that our moral lives are created and the level of morality in the world is defined.

It is important, too, to tell your children how you would react in that situation. Always remember that one key reason for the discussion is that you are their primary authority for what is right and wrong. What you say matters to them more than anyone else's opinion. How you respond to the scene, what you express as the "right" thing to do, has more influence on molding their character than anything else in their lives.

There are countless moments such as these that you can use to get your children thinking about the challenge of "doing the right thing." Point out how they feel when a kindness is done to them.

Remind them of how they feel when someone goes out of her way to help them solve a problem or make them feel more comfortable in a difficult social situation. Point out ethical actions in others, such as when a friend comes to comfort you during a time of loss or stress, or when a stranger comes after you to return an item you dropped in a store or on the street. Ethical behaviors such as these are available to everyone, every day. That is why it is so important to call them to your children's attention as examples of what it means to live life as an ethical human being.

Five Ways to Help Your Children Develop an Ethical-Action Consciousness

Everything teaches something. Your "teachable moments" may not always present themselves as ethical challenges, but your children will learn something from them just the same. Apart from role modeling (always the most important way), here are a few more techniques for motivating your children to think about moral issues:

1. Be an Ethical-Action Cheerleader

Acknowledging your children's positive behavior is something I've emphasized before and will emphasize again. Few learning experiences are as effective as being caught in the act of doing something right. Make sure your children know that you notice their ethical behavior. Look for opportunities to acknowledge their ethical decisions and praise them for their good moral judgment. When a child offers to help a younger sibling with homework or spontaneously does a favor for someone without expecting anything in return, such an act deserves recognition for bringing more kindness, caring, and love into the world.

2. Reinforce Integrity

Every day you spend with your children presents opportunities to teach lessons in integrity and trust. You can begin by giving them small, easily managed tasks, such as carrying silverware to the dinner table or putting laundry away, and then let the chores become increasingly complex as they grow older. The connection between doing chores and learning integrity lies within the context in which you assign the tasks. Every time your child completes an assigned task, tell him how proud you are that he can be trusted to keep his word and follow through on his commitments. This creates a link between integrity and earning the respect and admiration of loved ones. Any time you respond positively to a demonstration of trust is a moment that teaches the importance of trustworthiness.

Praise your children too when they resist a temptation for the sake of maintaining their integrity. This might involve returning a coveted object left at your home by a friend, returning change when a store clerk mistakenly gives them too much, behaving well when no one is around who might reprimand them for misbehaving, or otherwise doing the right thing when it might be convenient or emotionally less risky to do otherwise.

I believe that integrity forms a strong foundation on which other ethical values can be based. It is one of those qualities that no one can take away from us. Since young children can't conceptualize this important idea on their own, we must find appropriate ways to teach them what integrity is all about.

3. Use Your Children's Heroes as Teaching Examples

Integrity is one of the main ingredients of which children's media heroes are made—and so, for that matter, are courage, honor, altruism, and other positive ethical values. One good way to begin instilling these values in our children is to bring their attention to the way these values are naturally expressed by Batman, Nancy Drew, and other heroes from books, TV, and movies. Any time one of these heroes acts in a way you want your child to emulate can become a teaching moment. A simple comment like, "What I like about Steven Seagal's movies is that he always helps people in need," or, "Wasn't it nice in *Forever Young* how Mel Gibson fixed that family's roof and plumbing?" will get them thinking.

4. Find Teachable Moments in Popular Culture

Is the moral fiber of our children's generation being eroded by a constant bombardment of images from TV and rock music that glorify sex, violence, drugs, infidelity, even suicide? Though the particulars may differ, this issue in one form or another has engendered fierce debate for decades, even centuries. Just ask Socrates. We don't know for certain what influence popular culture has on children's worldview or lifestyle choice, but the question is not a trivial one when you consider the statistics: According to one of the more conservative estimates, the average adolescent from grades seven through twelve watches nearly 4,000 hours of television and listens to some 10,500 hours of rock music.

I believe that we do on some level become what we think about. That's why we must be very careful to fill our children's minds with inspiring thoughts and images of positive qualities. Doing this will help them to become, naturally and automatically, the kind of persons who exhibit these qualities.

Likewise, helping our children identify the negative messages they encounter in song lyrics or on TV will to some degree help mitigate the effect of these messages. For example, you might ask your children to share with you the words to some of their favorite rock songs, and then share your responses. Better perhaps is simply to ask them, after they have given you a copy of the words, what they think your impression might be. Their answers will reveal much about their attitudes toward the values you think are important, and about how effective you have been at instilling these values in them.

You can also sit with your children while they watch TV. Pay attention to the values implicit in their favorite programs. Ask them to notice the ways the heroes accomplish their goals—typically through physical force, bloodshed, revenge. Ask if there were other ways they might have chosen. Challenging your child to come up with a creative alternative is a great way to get her to consider a variety of options before making ethical decisions.

5. Nurture Your Child's Awareness of Self

Another important method for helping children become aware of ethical choices is to remind them to take the time to stop and think about their behavior. Most children, most of the time, act without examining what they're doing. To lead an ethical life, children must be taught the skill of stepping away emotionally from their actions, looking at them objectively, and making intelligent choices about whether or not they want to repeat them.

This ability to create an emotional distance between one's self and one's actions is a learned behavior. Here again, children can learn from your example. If they see you always justifying your actions, defending every decision you have made even after you've thought better of it, then children learn that "circling the wagons" and never admitting they are wrong is a high virtue.

It is far better for children to hear their parents rethink aloud decisions that they might have made in haste. It is far better for them to see that the adults whom they love and respect have the capacity to admit mistakes, to change their minds, and to examine choices and behavior from an objective, nondefensive position. Although this is not an easy thing to do, it is the best way to teach your children humility and moral self-examination, and that there is always an opportunity to improve one's behavior.

Instilling the Voice of Conscience

The point of all these teachable moments, the question that you want your children to ask themselves throughout their lives whenever they are confronted with an ethical choice, is "When this moment is over and I'm looking back on it in the future, will I be proud of the person I was and what I did?"

If you can instill this kind of reflective self-examination in your children when they are young, it will stay with them throughout their lives. They will always carry within themselves the still, small voice of conscience. It will remind them each day that they possess one of the most precious and irreplaceable gifts any human being can have: the gift of ethical behavior.

How to Recognize and Use "Teachable Moments"

■ Recognize that your children often learn moral lessons unconsciously, in casual moments.

■ Be aware of situations that represent ethical choices.

■ Talk with your children about the ethical challenges represented in everyday situations, the media, and popular culture.

■ Praise your children for their ethical choices.

■ Point out ethical behavior in others.

■ Let your children see your own thought processes regarding ethical decisions.

 *Leading Your Children to Ethical Choices in Everyday Life*

KEY #8

Have the Kind of Friends You Want Your Children to Have

I don't believe I have ever met a parent who did not on some level yearn for the ability to hand pick his or her children's friends. "Why," goes the lament, "does she continue to be friends with Susan [or John, or Sheila, or...] when all it does is cause her anxiety and grief?" Parents often find themselves comforting their children, drying tears of frustration or anger caused by the slings and arrows of outrageous friendship, and wondering whether there will ever be an end to the pain that ill-conceived peer relationships seems to cause.

This is not a trivial issue. Friendship choices are also ethical choices. The people with whom we associate, the people with whom we are comfortable, the various ways in which we relate to our friends all have a profound impact on the kinds of ethical decisions we make every day.

Think back again to your own childhood. Remember the impact your friends had on the choices you made? There were probably times when your friends' approval meant more to you than the approval or disapproval of your parents, or of anyone else. Peer acceptance was the measure by which you gauged much of your behavior, successes and failures. If a certain action, activity, manner of dress, or figure of speech was "cool" as far as your friends were concerned, it was okay by you as well.

Of course this social reality of childhood can give parents nightmares. They lament their inability to overcome the powerful pressure that peers exert on so many aspects of their children's lives. When all is said and done, however, it is a reality that every parent must accept.

This does not mean that you are powerless to influence your children's friendships. While you can't choose their friends, you can do something more vital—you can choose your own. You can make your friendships models for your children. You can have the kind of friends you'd like your children to have, and more importantly, you can *be* the kind of friend you would like your children to be.

The Futility of Dictating Friendships

The *least* productive way of influencing a child's choice of friends is to march into his room and announce, "From now on, you will not be allowed to spend any time with Michael." Ninety-nine percent of the time, it has the opposite effect to what you want.

Having "been there" as children, we all know this is true. In my own case, my parents' disapproval of my friends made being with them much more attractive and challenging. One "banned" friend and I would sneak out of our respective homes at three in the morning, hop on our bikes, meet at an agreed-on location, and have breakfast together at an all-night restaurant. Half the fun of it was knowing that my parents would have hit the ceiling if they ever found out.

Trying to dictate friendships to our children is an exercise in futility. Some things are simply beyond a parent's control. In truth, as parents, we don't always know who the "right" friends for our children are. Remember Eddie Haskell on the old "Leave it to Beaver" show, always the polite, thoughtful, ingratiating young man with Beaver's parents and just the opposite with his peers?

In my experience as a family counselor, most relationships that parents disapprove of eventually die out of their own accord. Most children are perceptive enough to make decisions about their friends that ultimately serve their best interests, even at the cost of a little security among their peers. When you raise your children to respect the values that are important to you, it becomes obligatory upon you in return to trust their judgment in return. Most of the time, when you have clearly articulated and modeled the ethical standards to which you aspire as a family, your children will rise to the occasion.

Your influence on your children's choice of friends will be mostly indirect, and your greatest success will come through the tried-and-true principle of modeling.

Modeling Your Own Friendship Choices

If you want to influence your children's friendships, take a look at your own. Think of the people you consider your friends. What qualities attracted you to them? How did you become friends? If you had it to do over again, would you still choose them as friends? Why, or why not? Could you present them to your children as models of ethical behavior? If you wanted to make new friends who reflected your core values, where might you find them?

These are important questions. Most people seem to drift into friendships accidentally, without much thought as to what they desire from their friends and what they are willing to give in return. Yet your friendships can have a powerful influence on your children's standards of behavior. This is why I believe you must consider every adult in your life who comes in contact with your children as though you have personally chosen him to lecture them on the subject, "Why you should be just like me."

In fact, this is very much what you are doing. As your children see you interacting with your friends, as they listen in on your conversations with them (which of course they do at every opportunity), they are absorbing complex lessons in social ethics.

Take a Critical Look at Your Friendships

When parents recognize the impact that their friendships have on their children, they often dissociate themselves from their friends' actions. They may realize on conscious scrutiny that Joe drinks heavily and makes a joke of it, that Jill has a habit of using racial slurs, that Sandy often talks gleefully about putting something over on someone in a business deal. Parents often tell me how embarrassed they have become to realize that long-term friends exhibit behavior that they now find offensive and don't want their children emulating.

Letting go of acquaintances of many years' duration is never easy. But it might be important for you to recognize that allowing certain people to be part of your life may send your children mixed messages about the attitudes and behaviors you feel are appropriate. If you decide to discontinue a friendship, consider explaining to your children that though this person has qualities you respect, there are compelling ethical reasons why you no longer want this person in your life. This teaches them that the decisions we make in life aren't permanent, but are part of a lifetime continuum of decisions that reflect the ethical quality of our lives.

How to Teach Your Children to Take Friendships Seriously

After modeling, the next-best thing you can do to influence your children's choice of friends may be to guide them toward the understanding of how important that choice can be.

Use your own friendships as a testing laboratory for your children's. Talk to your children about your friends: the reasons you value them as part of your life, the qualities you admire in them, the principle of give-and-take in relationships as it applies to you and your friends, and the social, emotional, and spiritual benefits that come through having these particular friendships. In this way, you teach your children something they otherwise might not realize—that they should not take friendships lightly; that they ought to put at least as much thought into choosing friends as they do into choosing the clothes they wear when they spend time with these friends.

Do not neglect to teach your children that sticking by our friends in the face of others' disapproval is also a worthwhile goal. We want our children to be loyal to people they care about, even as they make their year-by-year decisions about the moral character of those they choose to call their friends. But be sure to explain that a great many people in our world will judge us by the company we keep. They will come to conclusions regarding our integrity and personal qualities on the basis of whom we pick to be our friends.

No one would argue that such subjective character judgments are "fair." They aren't. But like it or not, that's the way real people make decisions about others in our world. Teach your children that there isn't much we can do about the judgment of others, but we can have a say about the extent to which we allow those others to influence our lives.

This is an extremely sophisticated concept, and I urge parents to present it to their children in just that light: "I'd like to talk to you about how your friends affect the kind of person you become and how others see you. This is a very mature, adult idea, but I think you can understand it. It's important for you to understand how your choice of friends can affect your life. As an adult, I have exactly the same experiences you do when it comes to choosing friends. I try to be aware all the time of how my friendships affect how I act and the kind of person I am."

Most children will not have the capacity to grasp this idea and its implications before adolescence. However, you can begin to express it to your children from the time they begin to question their choice of friends and comment negatively on their friends' behavior. If you have chosen your friends wisely, then it will be easier for you to illustrate this talk with your own example.

This is *not* to say that all friendships should be based on self-conscious, carefully planned criteria. We know they are not. Some people become our friends because we share common interests and experiences. Other friendships we just seem to fall into. It is still appropriate, however, as you approach this issue with your children, to examine all your friendships and see if they form an overall pattern of ethical behavior that you would be pleased to see your children re-create in their own lives.

We Have the Right to Choose Our Friends

Help your children become aware of the control that they have over their friendships, the choice they have either to nurture or to reject them. Children are often so insecure about themselves, so needy of acceptance and acknowledgment by their peers, that they will take anyone as a friend who offers them the appearance of friendship. When your children observe your friendships and understand the conscious choices you have made about them, they will come to realize that they have the power to make similar choices. This realization helps them develop the internal strength to seek out some friendships and to let go of others. It lets them feel that consciously choosing their friends is appropriate and praiseworthy. More importantly, it teaches them that they have an obligation to themselves to think consciously about their friendships and not simply to "fall in with the crowd."

Influencing Your Children's Choice of Friends

By expecting the same standards of yourself and your own friends that you want for your children, you exert an indirect influence over their choice of friends that is more effective than any direct control you may attempt. Another way of guiding them toward the friendships you feel are appropriate for them is to guide them toward weekend and after-school activities that are consonant with your values. If a child plays on a soccer team, participates in children's theater, or joins a church youth group with a community action program, it stands to reason that she will form friendships with other kids who are involved in the same groups.

This sort of "positive social engineering" can be the most effective way to subtly influence your children's friendship choices, at least before they reach late adolescence. As long as you still have some influence over their choice of activities, make a point of encouraging those you admire and discouraging those you don't. If you'd rather have your daughter get involved in a church group than go out for cheerleading, for example, call the parents of her current or potential friends and get them to encourage their children to participate as well. Offer to provide transportation to and from group events. Arrange carpools.

Share Stories from Your Childhood

Another way to influence your children's choice of friends is to share stories about your own childhood friendships. Talk about the positive friendships that were supportive and empowering, and the negative ones in which your naiveté was taken advantage of and your trust betrayed. Most children like to hear stories of their parents' childhoods. It can be liberating for them to discover that you were a real person who struggled with the same issues, insecurities and emotional pain that they are now confronting.

A mother once shared with me how she told her daughter about how deeply hurt she had been in junior high when the "popular" kids didn't include her in their group, and how often she had run home in tears because of it. Her daughter appeared disinterested while she was telling the story. Months later, however, after a particularly rough day at school, the girl repeated the story back to her mother and commented, "I guess if you lived through it, I can too. Those kids probably weren't worthy of your friendship anyway… and I don't suppose my so-called friends are either."

The mother was amazed that her daughter had stored her story away to be recalled when her own ego was under attack by the insensitivities of her "so-called friends." As she commented to me, "You never know when something you tell your children gets through."

She was right, of course. Stories about ourselves that we share with our children are like shiny pebbles on a seashore. We never know when a child might scoop one up to add to his collection, to be pulled out and admired with affection and delight on an emotionally rainy day. Sharing your stories is one of the best ways I know to create bonds between you and your children. It reassures them that you will be empathetic with their own struggles, because you've been there yourself.

Being the Kind of Friend You Want Your Children to Be

As with every other area of ethical development, "mentor modeling" is the key concept for your children's friendships—not just in choosing the type of friends you want them to have, but in *being* the kind of friend you want them to *be*.

The best way for your children to learn how to be a good friend is by watching and listening to you. How do you talk about your friends in front of your children? Do you speak of them with caring, respect, and support? Or do you put them down, express envy about their successes, and gloat about their disappointments? If your children acted like you do with regard to your friends, would their behavior please you, or would you try to change it?

Verbalize to your children those qualities in your friends that you admire, as well as trying to express them in your own behavior. This makes the process a conscious one. It lets your children understand that friendship is an aspect of life worth thinking about and planning. In this way, the process of choosing a friend takes on a much more concrete, substantial place in their understanding of the role of friendships in their lives.

 Giving Your Children Freedom to Choose

Again, it's helpful to remember that regardless of the friends you choose for yourself and the guidance you give your children, the decisions they make regarding the peers they bond with and the models they emulate will be theirs and not yours. You can influence and guide them in the hope that they will emulate your behavior, but their choices will ultimately be their own.

Despite this apparent lack of control, despite the anxieties you may feel over the negative influence of your children's peers, I can only advise you to trust your children. Trust that when all is said and done, they will make the right decisions. Trust that the values you have instilled in them have had sufficient impact on the core of their being to dispel any transitory effect the friendship-of-the-month might have. Though there certainly will be times when the esteem of their peers will weigh in more heavily with them than your own, the solid sense of right and wrong that they have learned from you will still be resting there underneath it all. All you need to do to remind yourself of this truth is to pause for a moment and consider your own need and desire, even now, for your parents' approval.

Of course it is important to pay attention to the friends your children choose and, if necessary, to guard your children from self-destructive behavior. But beyond protecting them from physical harm, remember that the process of growth and maturation inevitably involves painful lessons. Give your children the freedom to learn these lessons for themselves. After all, they will know that you will always be there when necessary to hold their hand or lend a sympathetic ear, to catch their tears, to give them your support and your unconditional love.

How to Influence
Your Children's Friendship Choices

■ Recognize that while you can influence your children's choice of friends, you cannot choose their friends for them.

■ Choose friends for yourself who reflect your core values.

■ Teach your children how their friendship choices affect others' judgment of their character.

■ Use indirect means to influence your children's choice of friends.

■ Help your children recognize that they have the power to choose their friends, and trust that in the long run they will make friendship decisions based on their values and best interests.

■ Show your children by your example what it means to be a good friend.

*Leading Your Children
to Ethical Choices
in Everyday Life*

KEY #9

Make Ethical Behavior a Family Affair

One of the least recognized of children's needs is the need to belong. We understand a child's needs for nourishment and shelter, for emotional and spiritual security; but we tend to overlook the need to feel connected with other human beings. This desire to belong is why people join organizations. It's why they feel such loyalty to their old schools, athletic teams, social clubs, and religious institutions.

Raising children of character requires us to create opportunities for them to feel this connection with others. Too often we think of ethical behavior only in personal, individual terms, and not as it applies to the wider context of community. When we teach our children the right way to act, it is because we live among other human beings. The most dangerous people in our world are the sociopaths who feel no connection to others, and who therefore find it easy to regard them as less than human. Only when children experience their lives as an integral part of the lives of others can they experience the deeply rooted sense of social responsibility that will make them ethical adults.

You can help your children meet this need by encouraging their participation in after-school activities, service clubs, and other group activities. You can join a church, synagogue, or other religious organization with a strong youth program. But the most effective way to nurture within your children this ethical and spiritual bond with the wider community is to participate *as a family* in activities that further the welfare of the community.

How to Meet the Challenge of Healing the World

The ultimate challenge of ethical parenting is to inspire children to view their relationship to the world as if they are personally responsible for how it turns out. For this to happen, they must experience their lives as connected to the lives of all people. They need to feel responsible for the quality of life on our planet, the well-being of society, and the fate of humanity. They need to appreciate that one of their goals as human beings is to bring a sense of completeness and fulfillment into the world.

In my spiritual tradition, this task is called "healing the world." It defines the primary goal of humanity as to join with God in completing the work of creation. This belief, that the higher power that created all life requires our partnership to renew creation on a daily basis, exists in many traditions, both religious and humanistic. It rejects the isolation of living for ourselves alone in favor of the responsibilities of being part of a family, a people and a community. It challenges us with the task of repairing our world (and certainly no one would argue that it isn't broken) and bringing it ever closer to the goal of wholeness and peace.

It is possible for everyone to participate in healing the world. It may even be the most important reason for being alive. More often than not, healing the world takes place in ordinary moments and simple gestures. We engage in this task by reaching out to others, righting wrongs, healing the shattered lives around us. We contribute to healing the world by bringing relief to the sick at heart, hope to those in despair, and material comfort to those in need.

Our responsibility to do what we can to fulfill this vision can be both exciting and challenging to our children. It requires that we identify concrete behaviors by which children can have a positive impact on their world. The more we can do this, the more we help them feel powerful and competent as ethical human beings.

One of the simplest ways of fulfilling this goal is to have a family "ethical homework assignment," in which you discuss with your children the social problems in the world and their possible solutions. Then together you will choose a task that will initiate your family's commitment to reach out to others. The important thing is to choose something concrete that you are actually able to accomplish. Refer to the **"Ethical Homework Assignment" charts on pages 150–151** to get your family interested and involved in healing the world.

If you make this an ongoing family activity, you can involve children of any age in the process. For example, you may decide to address one of the problems associated with the thousands of homeless children in our country. You might pledge to collect clothing from neighbors and bring it to a shelter that helps homeless families, or to volunteer to serve meals at the shelter one night each month for a year. All children who are of an age to understand the concept could go into their closets to find clothes or toys to share with children in need, or could participate in setting or clearing tables at the shelter.

A twelve-year-old I know chose a wonderful project. She turned her own birthday into an opportunity to bring joy into the lives of homeless families. Instead of having a party for herself, she got her whole family to cook food, bake cakes and cookies, and create party decorations, which they then delivered to a local family shelter. This child experienced the gift of joy that comes from meaningfully touching the lives of others. She learned in a firsthand, personal way the truth of the cliché that it is better to give than to receive.

Another child, a boy of fourteen, suggested that his family prepare sandwiches and other easily transportable food and drive around their city delivering it to homeless people on the streets. His personal act of healing the world soon inspired a community-wide effort and received the recognition of the President of the United States.

Here's another example: You might decide to pledge to help the environment, perhaps by alleviating the greenhouse effect in whatever small way you can. Your first activity might be to plant a tree for each member of your family. Children of all ages can participate in the activities necessary to fulfill this pledge: finding a location, choosing an appropriate kind of tree for that location,

Ethical Homework Assignment

What Can We Do to Heal the World?

1. Have a family meeting.

2. At the meeting, ask your children, "What do you think is wrong with the world?"

3. List all the ideas they come up with on a sheet of paper.

4. After your list is complete (you can always go back and add to it later), write each entry at the top of a separate sheet of paper.

5. Now have a brainstorming session. Consider in turn as many of the problems as you can, and have everyone suggest ideas for fixing it. Specify things that might be done to ease each problem by children, parents, teens, young adults, schools, government, religious and civic groups, neighborhoods, sports teams, teachers—anyone you might think of. The more inventive and unusual your solutions, the better. Brainstorming helps everyone go beyond the easy-to-think-of, ordinary solutions. Write each suggestion under the appropriate heading.

6. When your lists of solutions are complete (or when you need a break from compiling them), sit down as a family and select one approach with which to begin—something concrete, that you are actually able to accomplish.

7. Enter your solution on the Family Heal-the-World Pledge on the next page (or recreate the pledge on larger paper).

8. Agree on a timetable for implementing the pledge.

9. Have each family member sign the pledge (create individual pledges if you wish).

The Family
Heal-the-World Pledge

This is the first thing our family pledges to do to help heal the world:

_____

_____

_____

_____

_____

_____

_____

_____

_____

_____

We will try to accomplish this task by (date):

_____

Family member signatures:

_____

_____

_____

_____

_____

obtaining the tree, tools, and soil, and helping with the actual plant-ing. Your job is to join with your children while pointing out that they are fulfilling an important ethical value.

Ethical Action Can Transform Lives

Feelings of sensitivity and compassion in children do not spring up overnight. They result from growing up with parents who con-sistently express a conviction that all people are responsible for the welfare of one another. The girl who shared her birthday party with homeless children, for example, must have had wonderful parental role models to have come up with such a beautiful way of turning a potentially self-indulgent occasion into a life-transform-ing celebration.

There are endless possibilities for involving your family in projects that will contribute to healing the world while adding sat-isfaction and fulfillment to your own lives. Problems such as homelessness and environmental decline are likely to be with us for a long time. Here are a few other ways in which your children can participate in healing the world, either individually or with the entire family:

- Participate in a school or community trash pick-up, recy-cling, or graffiti-removal project.
- Participate in and solicit sponsors for a local "walk against hunger" or similar event.
- Spend time talking with or reading to residents at a home for the elderly.
- Bring small gifts to hospitalized children.
- Deliver meals to home-bound elderly or people with AIDS.
- Participate in service projects through community or civic groups.
- Collect medicine or other emergency needs for children in war-torn countries.

With a little creative thinking, you can come up with your own caring projects to serve as examples of ethical social action for your children. These projects do not have to be exotic or extravagant. Even the simplest acts, such as writing a letter as a family to civic officials or to the editor of a newspaper, can have a powerful and lasting effect on your children if they are set within the context of making the world a better place. All it takes is for you to recognize that children learn what they live, and to embrace healing the world as a value worth pursuing with actions that bring it to life.

Loving Others, Loving Yourself

A great paradox of raising emotionally healthy children is that while the experience of extending themselves to others can only grow out of a healthy self-esteem, their self-esteem in turn will be enhanced by experiences in which they see themselves as expressing esteem for others.

Consider the key principle expressed in the age-old maxim, "Love your neighbor as yourself." It's a simple idea, yet it contains one of the most sophisticated notions in our moral universe. Its obvious meaning seems to be to extend love to all humankind, but the real zinger in this phrase lies in the last two words. To love your neighbor as yourself, *you first have to love yourself.*

Every airline traveler is familiar with the standard flight attendant's lecture on emergency procedures, including the advice that when the oxygen masks drop down from the ceiling, "Please make sure that your own mask is securely fastened before assisting your children." Just as you must secure your own mask before you can be fit to render care to others, you must love yourself before you can be fit to demonstrate love for another person.

This, of course, is not an invitation to teach your child that self-centeredness and self-indulgence are okay. It's the issue of esteem once again. Psychologists affirm that individuals who are incapable of feelings of positive self-worth are equally incapable of loving anyone else. Selfish, demanding children are created when parents overindulge their whims and desires and withhold the kind of structure, limits, and discipline that children need. A strong foundation of "self-love," in the form of appreciating one's own worth and value, will help children grow up to be fully functioning, emotionally mature, caring adults.

Put Love-Your-Neighbor into Action

The mirror-image of the paradox is that children can raise their self-esteem through loving actions toward others. As we have observed, kids have a built-in sense of fairness. They continually find themselves frustrated by the discovery that life isn't fair. At almost any age, children have a natural compassion for others (especially other children) who are in need. Obviously, many adults feel the same way; that's why we commit ourselves to social action. But because we tend to think of childhood as being typified by self-centeredness, we are often surprised by the depth of passion and caring with which our children confront the plight of others. They know it isn't right for kids to go hungry, or for families to be caught in the crossfire of a war zone. By finding concrete, identifiable ways to address these unfairnesses, children reinforce their own self-worth and value as human beings.

It's up to you to give your children opportunities to live the value of "loving your neighbor." You don't teach it to them through grandiose thoughts or warm feelings about the unity of humankind. You can convey it only through your acts of compassion. Your children don't know what's really going on in your mind and heart. All they can know through direct experience is what you do.

It's hard to fool children. They have an aggravating habit of spotting the truth. There are few assertions more devastating to parents (or teachers, or spiritual leaders) than that we teach one standard and live another. I cannot emphasize too strongly or too often that our children will pay little attention to what we say unless it is consistent with what we do. If we want them to learn that being an ethical person means giving of ourselves to others, we must live this value ourselves.

♥ Having the Ability to Be a Moral Model

I realize that it is difficult for parents consciously to accept all the responsibilities they have brought upon themselves by becoming parents. The good news is that when it comes to influencing the way children perceive and act toward others, we have the ability as well as the responsibility.

Creating ethical family projects is a powerful learning experience that supports many of the other keys we've discussed in this book. It promotes self-esteem. It allows you to present yourself as a moral model. It creates teachable moments. It guides children in experiencing the truth of some of our most respected "words to live by." It involves children of all ages at a level appropriate to their moral understanding. Perhaps most significant of all, it shows your children that there are things you can do together as a family to reinforce the values that you cherish.

Successful ethical parenting involves communicating to our children that they can make a difference. It requires that they discover, with our help, that despite all the problems that afflict our world, they have the power to bring more light, joy, and love into even its darkest corners. Our challenge is to teach our children that when they look back on their lives, they will realize that the most important events were not written in the headlines, but in the small print of everyday encounters with human beings whose lives they touched.

How to Involve Your Children in Ethical Action in Your Community

■ Recognize that children need to feel connected with other human beings.

■ Create opportunities for your children to demonstrate ethical behavior in a community context.

■ Initiate family projects that contribute to healing the world.

■ Help build your children's sense of self-worth by inspiring them through your example to create their own caring social-action projects.

*Leading Your Children
to Ethical Choices
in Everyday Life*

KEY #10

Teach Your Children that Life Has Meaning

If I could teach my child only one lesson, it would be that her life has meaning. Only through appreciating the meaningfulness of their own lives can children truly realize that what they do matters, what they say matters, and who they are matters.

We have arrived at what may be the greatest challenge in ethical parenting: to inspire your children with the faith that there is ultimate meaning to their lives. Most of the time we seem to live from day to day, caught up in our routine, focused on little more than the immediate moment. It's easy to lose sight of the loftier vision to which we can aspire. If we can communicate that vision, if we can grasp with both hands the certainty that there are higher purposes in life and lovingly pass it on to our children, we will have done our job as parents.

As You Think, So Shall You Become

On the most basic, functional level, life has meaning if we live it as if it does. If our children live their lives as if they can bring meaning and purpose into the world each day, then that's exactly what will happen. They will discover their own meaning and purpose in the process of life itself.

I believe I know the secret to finding that meaning. I can state this with confidence and with all humility because it's not a secret I discovered myself. It has been part of many spiritual traditions, and for thousands of years has served people as a key to joy, fulfillment, and satisfaction. You'll find it not only in ancient sacred writings but in corporate management seminars and in hundreds of contemporary motivational books and tapes designed to inspire people to maximize their "human potential."

In its most direct form, this secret is expressed as follows: *"As you think, so shall you become."*

Another way to state it is: *"What the mind can conceive and believe, the mind can achieve."*

In all the world's cultures, across countless generations, for men and women in all walks of life, this idea has been the key to success. It is the idea behind every political movement, every technological invention, every philosophical idea or artistic achievement. Everything that has ever been created by human effort began as a vision in the mind of a single individual.

This is why we must teach our children to embrace life as an experience filled with endless possibilities. This attitude encourages creative thinking, empowers emotional and spiritual growth, and opens the mind to the potential of transforming the world. It is our responsibility to excite our children's minds with the possibility of a more perfect world, to inspire them to do their part to make that world a reality, and to teach them that the quality of their world will relate directly to the quality of their own contribution to it.

We Are Like Pebbles in a Pond

In one sense, none of us actually lives in "the world." We live within tiny, interlocking circles of relationships. It is within these circles of family, friends, acquaintances, co-workers, colleagues, and the strangers we encounter that our behavior has the greatest impact. All human life is made up of circles like these, interacting with one another and rippling out into the world. When we live in ways that create meaning and positive value, our actions, like pebbles tossed into a pond, will send out ripples that influence the lives of others far outside our circles.

How to Give Your Children the Power of a Positive Attitude

Not only do your children get to determine the quality of their lives through their choice of behavior, they also get to determine how they respond to circumstances of their lives that they didn't choose. This is because when it comes to the choices that make life meaningful, the most important ingredient is *attitude*.

There is a famous quote attributed to Thomas Edison: "I discovered a thousand ways not to make an electric light bulb." It was Edison's remarkable, consistent, positive attitude, his conviction that he would succeed even after a thousand failures, that was largely responsible for his phenomenal record of success. Your children could hardly choose a better role model for patterning their attitude about life.

As parents, we must instill this attitude of positive expectation in our children. No, it doesn't matter whether a child becomes a famous inventor (doctor, rocket scientist, symphony conductor, railroad conductor, teacher, athlete, tree-trimmer, or taxi driver). What matters is that whatever misfortune may befall her in her life, she will be able to encourage herself to transform her adversity into something positive.

In fact, it is our attitude that largely determines whether we *experience* life as positive or negative. It is our attitude, not the circumstances of our life, that determines how we feel about ourselves and our world. It is our attitude that leads us to feel competent to take control of our life. It is our attitude that lets us feel fulfilled. It is our attitude that can transform frustration into excitement, disappointment into anticipation, failure into success.

Goals, Dreams, and Visions Can Sustain Life

A dramatic illustration of the power of attitude is found in the work of Dr. Viktor Frankl. A world-renowned psychiatrist, Frankl was interned in the Auschwitz death camp during World War II. Observing thousands of people struggling to survive under the most brutal and dehumanizing of circumstances, Frankl became fascinated with the question of why some of these people lived and others died. When he was liberated from the camp, he resolved to dedicate the rest of his life to the pursuit of this knowledge.

In his profoundly moving book, *Man's Search for Meaning,* Frankl shares his discovery of the most important factor that determined which prisoners survived and which perished. He found that the power of an individual's will to live was grounded in a conviction that there was *something worth living for*—a goal, a dream, a vision that was greater than the self. In some cases, the goal was to be reunited with a loved one. In others, it was to fulfill some lifelong ambition. In still others, it was simply the desire for revenge against the Nazis. In all cases, however, the key that separated one group from the other, the force that kept people alive in these extreme circumstances of degradation and utter powerlessness, was this driving internal sense of mission.

I share Viktor Frankl's story with you as a way of illustrating that the principle is the same whether the goal is life itself or "merely" the fulfilled life that is every parent's goal for his or her children. It's not circumstances that determine success or failure—not even in Auschwitz. No matter what adversity may befall your children, it will ultimately be their attitude that determines its impact on their lives.

Time and again, in over twenty years of counseling families when trauma, tragedy, frustration and failure invade their lives, I have had the privilege of witnessing the remarkable recovery of family relationships, the healing of lives, the turning of tragedy into triumph and of despair to renewal. I believe that none of these miraculous turnarounds could have been accomplished without an attitude of hope in the future, of faith in people's ability to change, grow, and make a difference.

Give Your Children the Gift that Really Keeps On Giving

This is why I believe that one of the most lasting gifts you can give your children is this positive mental attitude. I believe that this quality more than any other is the source of fulfillment and satisfaction in the heart of every successful person. What makes the idea so powerful is that it places in your children's own hand the primary responsibility for control over their lives.

This is truly a gift that keeps on giving. As a parent, you cannot protect your children from life's misfortunes, no matter how hard you try. You cannot be there every moment to watch and protect. You cannot determine their diet or hold their hand every time they cross the street. You can't control their choice of friends or their choice of mates. In a sense, to be a parent is a lifelong experience of holding your breath and letting go.

What *is* in your power is to do everything you can during your children's crucial growing years to give them the expectation that they can positively affect the quality of their lives. The events of life are transitory. It's your children's attitude toward those events that will have an impact on their lives. You can teach them that even when circumstances seem out of their control, their response to those circumstances is *always* under their control.

Absolute Powerlessness Corrupts Absolutely

If I seem to be belaboring this concept, it's because there is a close correlation between the sense of control and ethical behavior. The feeling of powerlessness, of having no determination over the course of one's life, is devastating and debilitating. It can cause people to rationalize all sorts of negative behavior: "I have no control; therefore what I do doesn't matter. *I* don't matter." It's the people who feel this way who are responsible for most of the violent, antisocial acts that plague our world. When we help our children develop a positive mental attitude, we give them the tools they need to transcend this feeling.

You already know how to do this: by giving your children opportunities to demonstrate and feel their competence. Give them tasks that they can perform well, assign them responsibilities that build their sense of accomplishment, and you will be doing more for them than all the academic knowledge than they could possibly acquire.

Measuring Your Children by Moral Standards

At the same time, do not forget that your children need to know by your words and actions that you accept, respect, and appreciate them for their inner value, not merely for their external accomplishments. They must observe again and again that you measure the worth of others by the strength of their character, not by the size of their house, their car, or their bank account. If you judge others by their material success, your children will naturally assume that you measure their own worth and value by the same standards.

The key is to link your admiration of ethical values in others to your expectations for your children. Judge them by the same standards as you judge others. Acknowledge them for actions that show compassion for others and for choices that indicate moral reasoning, not for the "accomplishments" that have to do merely with the accumulation of things.

A prime example of how parents can inadvertently focus on external accomplishments is the issue of grades. High marks in school can become a commodity prized as a medium of exchange, to be traded for money or privileges. My personal feeling is that paying children for getting good grades devalues the experience. By taking grades out of the realm of personal achievement and reducing them to objects of the marketplace, we teach children that life is a barter game.

I would prefer that children value their accomplishments for their own sake. I would want them to know that grades are symbols of their dedication. I would rather reward them for having the integrity to follow through with a specific commitment to themselves, their teachers, or their parents about the quality of their schoolwork—a certain number of study hours, for example, or an exercise of good judgment such as staying home to finish an assignment instead of going out with their friends. This way, the reward focuses not on the grades themselves but on the qualities of character they symbolize. It is on these qualities that we want our children to base their sense of personal worth—not on what they get, but on how they see themselves in relation to others.

Our Value Lies in What We Give

This is the fundamental truth behind the cliché, "It is better to give than to receive." Most people interpret this saying as expressing a kind of mild altruism, whereby one "should" feel happier about giving gifts than getting them. What it really teaches is the difference in fundamental self-worth between the "givers" and "takers" of the world. The givers are those whose approach to others is, "How can I make a difference in your life, what can I add to it, how can I make it better?" There are few grander feelings than knowing that you have done something to touch another person's life. It is this sense of giving that the aphorism refers to, not to the bestowing of physical presents.

The takers of the world are those who see life from the perspective of need, want, and scarcity. They perceive the world as children might regard a box of candy being passed around a bustling living room. The children know that if they don't act quickly and assertively in their own self-interest, there won't be any candy left by the time the box gets around to them.

Life for many people is a game of grab-the-candy-box. If these people were able to see life as being primarily about love and not about things, they would be a lot less anxious about loss. Love comes in an unlimited supply, unlike a box of candy—which, significantly, often serves as a symbol of love. It's too easy for children (and adults) to feel that when the symbol is gone, so is the love. This is one reason why they so aggressively pursue the symbols—money in trade for grades, boxes of candy, cars, jewelry.

Others, however, recognize that the symbols are external, while the love comes from a much more profound, limitless place. Raising children of character means creating the kind of family life in which your children learn firsthand the difference between love and its symbols—the distinction between doing the right thing for its own sake and doing it for external rewards.

Three Techniques for Creating an Environment of Love

In the end, all your authority as a parent is based on love. Without your love, demonstrated in a multitude of ways every day, you will never establish and maintain an authentic foundation of positive influence with your children.

As we have seen, two key ways in which we communicate our love for our children are time and focus. When we give someone our time, that rare and unrenewable commodity, it can't help but make him feel significant in your sight. When we give someone our undivided attention, it communicates the powerful emotional message that she is worthy of our notice.

This is why simply making ourselves available to listen to our children is such a powerful parenting tool. All children need hugs, emotional as well as physical. Listening to our children, giving them our full one-on-one attention, is the simplest way of letting them know that we are on their side.

Often there is nothing we can do to ease their pain or make the problem go away. We can't always ride in on a white charger to be their champion. But we can give them the certainty of knowing we are behind them, that we care, that we will always be there for them. This certainty, this unshakable knowledge of our love and support, gives them the foundation to discover the inner strength they need to vanquish their own dragons.

An environment of love is an environment of meaningfulness. Although there is no "magic pill" for teaching your children to appreciate that life has purpose, there are several practical, everyday techniques you can use to create a supportive, loving environment that will lead them toward that appreciation.

Technique 1: Actively Encourage Your Children

Help your children pursue those activities, relationships, and involvements that will help them build confidence. Every child has areas of strength and weakness. Every child is drawn more to some activities and experiences than to others. Successful parents actively encourage their children to pursue activities they enjoy, even if they themselves find these interests incomprehensible. Too many parents push their children into tennis, soccer, ballet, or piano lessons simply because they have decided that "it's good for them." This is a surefire prescription for resentment and disaster. Many years may go by before an individual will even consider trying an activity he was forced to endure as a child.

Helping children discover what they do like is always more effective than forcing them to do what they don't like. Actively encouraging participation in activities that give your children pleasure is one of the best ways I know to ensure that they will feel good about themselves and therefore about life itself. And since we all enjoy doing things that we're good at, your children's participation in activities they like is inevitably a self-validating, confidence-building experience as well.

Technique 2: Exercise Verbal Self-Control

Whoever came up with the childhood taunt "Sticks and stones may break my bones but words will never hurt me" must have been comatose throughout his childhood! Broken bones mend relatively quickly, but a self-image shattered by angry words or sarcastic put-downs may never be whole again. Words are among the most powerful weapons in the parental arsenal. They can make a child feel like a star or like the most worthless human being on earth.

Too often, parents are oblivious to the potentially devastating power of their words. Every one of us can remember words spoken by parents or teachers that crushed us emotionally and undermined our sense of self-worth. Until the age when children begin the process of individuation, of separating themselves emotionally from their parents, Mom and Dad are the ultimate authority for everything in life. Being a parent is almost a godlike state—whatever you say is the truth.

Verbal self-control means "watching your mouth." I don't mean by this that an occasional negative word spoken in anger will destroy a child's self-esteem. We all "lose it" every now and then. I think there are times when disapproval passionately expressed can communicate to our children our love for them and our deep concern for their well-being. What really destroys a child's ability to see meaning and purpose in life is a pattern of consistent verbal abuse. It can be as destructive as placing a child in isolation, for it conveys the same message—that they are not worthy of your love.

Verbal self-control means setting standards and limits for your own behavior as well as for the behavior of your children. It demonstrates the value of respect. It models the kind of behavior you expect from them. Even something as simple as saying "please" and "thank you" to your children communicates that you see them as human beings of worth and value, regardless of their age.

Verbal self-control means making decisions in advance. It means deciding with your parenting partner what kind of verbal messages you want to communicate to your children, and what kind you want to avoid. After you have made this determination, it is easier to identify the specific words and phrases you do and do not want to use when reprimanding your children.

Sit down with your partner and complete the **"Verbal Self-Control Guide" on page 170**. First, list the goals that you want your children to achieve as a result of your parenting decisions: their sense of self-worth, their sense of social responsibility, and their specific behaviors in interacting with peers, authority figures, and other adults. Next, write down the specific positive language you want to use consistently with your children to help them achieve the respective goals you have listed. Finally, list all the insulting terminology, belittling phrases, and humiliating expressions you want to avoid using with your children. This list can be a handy reference guide to review now and then. Some parents I know read through their list at least once a day to keep the positive and negative phrases fresh in their mind. None of us is perfect, and there will be times when you slip. But having a handy list of verbal "do's" and "don'ts" can be helpful in reinforcing the best within yourself and within your children.

Technique 3: Teach Your Children that They Make a Difference

Never miss a chance to teach your children that they make a difference in the world. Encourage independence and self-expression. Create a home environment in which everyone speaks freely about the important issues in their lives. Show your children that they are worthy of your respect by listening to their opinions, perhaps even by allowing their ideas to change your way of doing things every now and then. At every level of childrearing, respect and love go hand-in-hand. If your children feel respected by you, they can't help but feel secure in your love as well.

Take every opportunity to remind your children of their uniqueness. So often children long to be someone else—the girl down the block who has so many friends, the football star, the kid who seems so effortlessly to get straight A's, the child who always acts so self-assured. It is hard for children to comprehend that however they may struggle to be someone else, they can never be better than the original—and at the same time, no one could ever possibly be better at being "them" than they themselves.

That's why it's so important to help your child realize and appreciate the miracle of her own uniqueness. Of all the billions of human beings who have ever lived or ever will, she is one of a kind. She is the only "she" there could ever be, and as such, her task while she is on this beautiful planet is simply to be the best "she" that she can possibly be.

Verbal Self-Control Guide

Verbal Communications Goals

Behavior and self-esteem goals I want my children to achieve as a result of my communication with them:

_____

_____

_____

_____

_____

_____

Words to Use

Positive language I will use consistently to help my children achieve these goals:

_____

_____

_____

_____

Words to Avoid

A reminder list of negative words and phrases I do not wish to use with my children:

_____

_____

_____

_____

_____

Being the Adult Your Child Can Grow Up to Be

As we come to the end, I wish to remind you one last time of the running theme of this book: the power of personal example. If I could summarize this book in one sentence, I would say, simply, *Be the kind of person you want your children to become.* I truly believe that if everyone followed this advice, this book and others like it would be entirely superfluous.

It is a great and demanding challenge to measure yourself by the same standards of ethical behavior, character, and personal worth by which you measure your children. If you cannot feel good about yourself with regard to your values, your integrity, how you treat others, and the contributions you make to the life of your community, how can you expect ethical behavior of your children?

Have the Courage to Care

It takes courage, optimism, and profound faith to undertake the task of raising ethical children. To do so even with the realization of how much is beyond your control is truly an act of great love. It would be easy to throw up your hands in despair and give in to the pervasive influences of materialism, consumerism, and instant self-gratification. When in spite of it all you persist in learning all you can, overcoming frustration, and doing your best to create a legacy of values and moral behavior, you ought to feel proud of your commitment and dedication.

The very fact that you care, that you have taken the time to develop an awareness of the attitudes, behaviors, and skills necessary to give your children this gift, is a tribute to your faith in yourself, your children, and the future of our world. Every time you teach your children by word and deed what it is to be an ethical human being, you boldly declare that the actions of a single individual really do make a difference. And this lesson is important enough to be taught again and again until it is shared by every person on our planet.

As we have seen throughout this book, there are no magic answers, no money-back guarantees, no unassailable techniques. Yet I believe absolutely that life has meaning and purpose that you can discover together with your children. I believe that you can help bring your children to awareness of their own power to make a difference in the world around them. I have shared with you many concepts and practical techniques for inspiring them to discover that meaning. Know for certain that if every parent on earth were as dedicated to raising children of character as you are, then the world would become all it can be.

So: Have the courage to be imperfect. Have the courage to make mistakes and to admit your errors in judgment. Have the courage to believe that despite your imperfections, your children will still love you. Have the courage to include your children in the important decisions of your life. And have the courage to believe through it all that they will grow up to be emotionally healthy, compassionate, ethical human beings. If you do, then every day will be a cause for celebration, and the world our children will create together will be a world of moral vision, a world of love, and a world of peace.

How to Influence Your Children to Embrace the Meaningfulness of Their Lives

- Recognize that we give our lives meaning through an attitude of positive expectation.

- Teach your children to embrace life as an experience filled with endless possibilities for positively affecting the quality of their lives and for transforming the world.

- Help your children experience their competence, but focus your acknowledgment and praise on their ethical actions and growth.

- Inspire and encourage your children to ethical behavior through demonstrations of your love.

- Never miss a chance to help your children realize that they make a difference in the world.

- Live your life as the kind of adult you want your children to grow up to be.

Afterword:

The Roots
of Our Ethics

This book was designed to share some of the major ideas that form the foundations of our ethics. I have based the book on the assumption that there is an ethical standard to which all human beings must be held if the world itself is to survive. For example, consider this simple list of principles, or "rules to live by," we are likely to agree on as ethical:

1. Regard freedom as a basic human right.
2. Don't pursue values that degrade your humanity.
3. Be someone that others can count on.
4. Take control of your own life, to make it meaningful.
5. Treat members of your family with honor, respect, and dignity.
6. Honor the sanctity of human life.
7. Create loving, trusting relationships.
8. Don't steal.
9. Don't lie.
10. Appreciate what you have.

Does this list sound vaguely familiar, like an old friend encountered years later on the street? If you ask most people who have grown up in the Western world to identify the foundations of their ethics, they will probably cite this list—even if they cannot name more than two or three of the items on it. It is upon these principles that all subsequent ethical commentary in our culture has been based. For your purposes in raising ethical children, these ten principles can serve as excellent guidelines for a basic list of universal ethical values.

In case you haven't recognized them, here is the way they are usually stated:

1. I am your God who brought you out of the land of Egypt, out of the house of slavery.
2. You shall have no other Gods besides me.
3. You shall not use God's name in vain.
4. Remember the Sabbath day to keep it holy.
5. Honor your father and mother.
6. You shall not murder.
7. You shall not commit adultery.
8. You shall not steal.
9. You shall not bear false witness against your neighbor.
10. You shall not covet your neighbor's house, your neighbor's wife... or anything else that is your neighbor's.

Understanding Our Ethical Values

Stating "The Ten Commandments" in a nonreligious context reminds us again that our ethical system is founded upon the Judeo-Christian tradition, whether or not we profess a religious belief system. It also reminds us of what these rules to live by actually teach. They offer guidelines for developing the qualities that allow the human community to function at its best. They form a blueprint for creating the ideal social order—which, after all, is what ethics is all about. Let's take a closer look at these age-old principles, see if we can come to an understanding of them beyond what you may have learned in church or synagogue, and learn how you can impart this understanding to your children.

The First Commandment: Acknowledge Universal Moral Principles

The first commandment doesn't seem to "command" us to do anything. "I am your God who brought you out of the land of Egypt, out of the house of slavery." Most religious teachers over the years have understood it as an indirect command to believe in God, yet it doesn't say anything about belief at all.

I see it rather as a *challenge* to belief in a "higher power," an ultimate source of creation and of judgment between right and wrong. The Israelites were slaves in Egypt, and at a particular moment they walked to freedom. This is why Jewish tradition celebrates freedom as humanity's most basic "God-given" right. Since nearly every people has experienced oppression and liberation during its history, this association of freedom with Godliness has become a universal message of Western ethics.

This, to me, is why the Ten Commandments begin with the idea that "God" is the power that transforms our lives from those of slaves to those of free human beings. The First Commandment is really a call to insist on freedom as a fundamental right, and to recognize the spark of freedom in every human spirit as the spark of the universal spirit.

It is possible to teach this idea to your children without the religious context. But if they are to grow up to be ethical people, they must recognize that we human beings are not the be-all and end-all of life. They must understand that there are forces in the universe, whatever we choose to call them, that are much greater than ourselves, and which we can use as sources of inspiration and awe. They must grow up with an appropriate sense of their place in the universe, a tempering of their tendency to arrogance, an understanding of the importance of humility.

Show your children pictures of the earth taken from space. Ask them to point out the boundaries that distinguish one country from another. Join in their "Aha!" when they realize that there are no boundaries except as we human beings have artificially imposed them. This is a primary lesson in the oneness of humanity: All that divides us are our fears and insecurities.

Your shaping of your children's everyday actions will not by itself result in ethical behavior. It must also come from a deeper sense of connection to all life and responsibility for the quality of our world, a realization that we are only a tiny drop in the vast sea of the cosmos. Your children can learn to recognize their place in the universe through their experiences as human beings, the beauty of a flower, the inspiration of love, the strength of courage—and the act of personal liberation. It is this recognition that gives relevance and power to the idea of universal ethical laws.

The Second Commandment: Avoid Idolatry

"You shall have no other Gods besides me" does not refer only to the worship of images or belief in exotic religions. For us today, idolatry can mean anything that assumes such importance in our lives that it diminishes our ethical values. It is just such "false gods" that we want to teach our children to avoid.

Consider addictions, for example. When we fall prey to alcohol, drugs, food, gambling, or any other self-destructive compulsion, we have effectively elevated these habits to the level of "gods." They become the motivations of our thoughts and actions, the driving force in our lives.

Or, consider greed. The Bible does not teach us that "money is the root of all evil," only that the *pursuit* of money can cause grief to everyone around us by blinding us to the values that are truly important. When money becomes not a means to an end but an end in itself, it takes on the status of a false god.

It's no coincidence that "the me decade" (the 1970s) was followed by "the decade of greed" (the 1980s). The idolatry that greed represents also finds expression in the self-indulgence that has become all too commonplace in our culture. Too many people act as if excess were the same as excellence, as if the more we consume, the more we demonstrate our value as human beings.

"You shall have no other Gods besides me" is a lesson in the importance of avoiding idol-worship of all kinds. If it had been written in our time, it might cry, "Stay sober; take care of your body, mind, and spirit; fill your thoughts with positive, life-affirming ideas every day." The Second Commandment reminds us that all excesses, whether in the form of mind-altering substances, money, status, or celebrity worship, diminish our children's ability to live their lives according to the values that matter.

You teach these values to your children by living them yourself. If you take drugs, drink alcohol daily, indulge in talk about how much money you are making or hope to make, complain about how you are falling short of your material goals, or act as if the accumulation of things is your ultimate purpose in life, you are instilling idolatry in your children.

Here is a project you can do with your family that has the goal of identifying the important things of life: Have each person write down what he or she considers to be the three most important things in your home. (Children who are too young to write can make an oral list.) Compare notes. Ask what would happen if those things were destroyed in a fire. How crucial are they to your family? If you were to lose them, how would it really affect you?

Now have everyone write down the three most important "things" in your home that aren't *things:* people, relationships, feelings, personality traits and so on. Ask your children to imagine how different your lives would be if *these* were missing. It becomes immediately obvious where your true values lie. Even small children will understand that it is more important to have love, laughter, and freedom than the latest computer game or the doll that turns into a flying machine.

The Third Commandment: Have Integrity

"You shall not use God's name in vain" is often misunderstood as a ban on swearing, particularly on using the word "god" in a nonreligious sense (as in "goddamn"). The real meaning refers to an ancient practice of calling upon God as one's authority when making a vow or pledge. It's rather like raising your right hand and saying "so help me, God" when taking the oath to tell the truth in a court of law. If you do this with no intention of keeping your pledge, you are using God as spiritual collateral when in fact you are lying, thereby degrading the image of God.

The Third Commandment, therefore, is a call to integrity. It is an admonition to be someone that others can count on, someone whose "yes" is a yes, and whose "no" is a no. It is a warning not to use God's name falsely or frivolously in making promises—"God" here representing your highest and most important values. If you are willing to denigrate these values by using them to lie to others, you are obviously not worthy of anyone's trust.

As you know, your children learn integrity by seeing you demonstrate it in your dealings with others. You can reinforce this lesson by insisting that your children keep their word and by making them aware of those inevitable times when they (and you) are let down by others who come up short in the integrity department. When this happens, point out how disappointed you are, how disheartening it is to live in a world where you can't depend on people to mean what they say, and how much you respect and admire those people in your life who are worthy of your trust.

There are ample opportunities to demonstrate to your children the difference between integrity and its absence. Praise them every time they follow through on a promise, even in such routine matters as going to bed at a particular time or finishing their homework before turning on the TV. The specifics don't matter. What's important is that you show them how proud you are every time they demonstrate integrity and trustworthiness. Never miss a chance to reinforce how important this quality is to you and how crucial it is for making the world a better place to live.

The Fourth Commandment: Make Life "Holy"

What does "holiness" really mean? In our spiritual tradition, it is something reflected in the action of human beings, but it does not have anything to do with meditation or cutting one's self off from the world. It means acting in such a way as to bring our highest values and noblest ideals into play in our everyday lives. The Fourth Commandment can be a tool to teach your children about taking control of that which is in their power, and about not allowing outside forces to dictate the quality of their lives.

"The Sabbath" can be a symbol for achieving this mastery over our lives. It is a reminder of our consciousness. Unlike animals, who have no choice but to act in accordance with genetically programmed instincts, we humans have the power to make conscious choices about most of the important matters in our lives. "Remember the Sabbath day to keep it holy" can mean creating time to contemplate who we are and who we wish to become.

The best way to teach your children these values is to guide them in making intelligent choices. Begin when they are young by giving them alternatives from which to choose and praising them for their positive, constructive choices. As they mature, help them create a structure that allows for work, play, school, and outside activities while pointing out the importance of having this balance in their lives. Try to place an ethical context, like a frame, around their everyday experiences. When you catch your child helping someone else, for example, make a point of telling him, "I'm proud of you when you show concern for others," or "Thank you for helping to make the world a better place."

It is important for children to recognize that they have the ability to make their life special—"holy," if you will. When they give of themselves, or even when they set aside time to view a beautiful sunset, they are bringing holiness into their lives.

The Fifth Commandment: Create Family Harmony

"Honor your father and mother" is not merely an admonition to show respect for one's parents. It is a statement about the importance of family harmony, about our responsibility to treat family members with respect and dignity. It is a reminder that the family is the center and foundation of society, which can only function effectively when children can experience emotional stability and demonstrate respect for those who shaped the world they have inherited.

In many ways, respect is at the core of all moral social behavior. It is the value behind what may be the best known of all ethical standards: "Do unto others as you would have others do unto you." The so-called "Golden Rule" is a formula for respect that goes hand-in-hand with the Fifth Commandment. If you want to create an ethical environment in which your children respect you, show

respect for them. If they don't feel worthy enough as human beings to deserve your respect, it is impossible for them to internalize the need to respect others. This is true at any age, but it is
particularly so with teenagers. You need to demonstrate in your
daily interactions with them that you respect their opinions. You
must learn to strike a balance between asserting your authority
when warranted and showing your respect for them by allowing
them the freedom to make choices.

Another direct way to reinforce this value in your children is
by demonstrating respect for *your* parents. When you send your
parents a birthday or anniversary card, for example, explain to
your children that it's important even for adults to honor their parents. Any time your children show respect for you, even by the
simplest act of courtesy or thoughtfulness, take the opportunity to
commend them for honoring the harmony of your family.

The Sixth Commandment: Honor Human Life

"You shall not murder" is usually mistranslated as "You shall not
kill." Most people would agree that murder is not the same as killing. Most codes of ethics—including the tradition from which these
Commandments come—exempt or even condone killing in self-
defense. Most also acknowledge the inevitability of war.

In any event, what does this commandment have to do with raising children? Most of us (thankfully!) do not have to go to any special
lengths to demonstrate to our children that murder is morally wrong.

Our concern is the deeper implications of "Don't murder." Our
job as parents is to teach our children to respect the sanctity of
human life, to value every human being as one who carries within
a "spark of the divine." Murder (and war) ultimately come about
because one person is able to see another as somehow less human
than he or she. The "enemy" is always spoken of in degrading
slang that robs them of their humanity and distances us emotionally from them. "Kraut," "jap," and "gook" (also "nigger," "spick,"
"bitch," "pig," "faggot," "bum," and the like) are words that make
human beings seem not human at all, and therefore easier to kill.

The Sixth Commandment therefore can be a reminder that all people share the same hopes, dreams, frustrations, and desires, no matter what their color, gender, language, religion, nationality, or station in life. Teach your children not only to respect people who are different but to find out what they can learn from them as well. Stop them from using dehumanizing slang terms for any group of human beings. Don't laugh at, tell, or permit others to tell derogatory ethnic jokes in your presence. By following these guidelines, you teach your children the dignity of all people and, ultimately, why we are forbidden to murder another human being.

The Seventh Commandment: Be Committed

"You shall not commit adultery" is naturally assumed to be a topic for adults only. What underlies the Seventh Commandment, however, is the importance of family stability—the institution of marriage, yes, but any other committed, loving relationship as well. Too many people in our world are raised in families where there is precious little trust. Children need boundaries and a structure they can depend on. They need parents who give them unconditional love, who increase their store of self-esteem, who build a world around them that is safe and secure. If you emphasize the importance of trusting relationships when your children are small, they are much more likely to commit themselves to such relationships when they reach adulthood.

You lay the foundation for such relationships by modeling and teaching integrity, commitment, and follow-through as these qualities are expressed in your children's relationships with others. A child demonstrates integrity every time she keeps her word to a friend or shows up for a date on time. A child learns the impact of a lack of commitment when a friend who has made an agreement to work on a homework assignment with him backs out at the last minute. Any such occasion can be a teaching opportunity, a chance for you to reinforce with your children that our commitments to each other really matter, a reminder that each of us has a profound impact on the lives of our family and friends.

The Eighth Commandment: Respect the Rights of Others

For many children (and adults), "You shall not steal" is a self-esteem issue. Stealing can be a reflection of an inner neediness that stems from insecurity, tension, anxiety, and fear. Laying claim to things that belong to others can be a negative way of trying to exert control over one's own environment.

The Eighth Commandment can be a tool for teaching respect for the rights of others in an otherwise "me-first" world. For the youngest children, a straightforward this-for-that is appropriate: You don't steal because you wouldn't want others to steal from you. As children get older, you can teach them that the reason stealing is wrong is because we are responsible for creating the kind of world in which we want to live, a world of trust, justice, dignity, and compassion. To create such a world requires that we act in every way to bring the real world closer to that ideal.

The Ninth Commandment: Preserve Trust through Truth

Like the previous two Commandments, "You shall not bear false witness" reminds us of the central role of integrity in interpersonal relationships. Contained within these simple, straightforward messages are the fundamental principles necessary to establish order, security, and human dignity, whether between loving partners, neighbors, or parents and children.

"Bearing false witness," in children's language, is "lying." If you rephrase the Ninth Commandment as "Don't lie," it is immediately clear how relevant this issue is to children's lives. Almost every child lies now and then. Their "false witness" might be as relatively harmless as claiming to have finished their homework or denying having eaten the last piece of cake in the refrigerator. For children, lying is often a test of the adult world's tolerance of, and latitude toward, unacceptable behavior. It's one of the ways kids probe for limits and ask (albeit unconsciously) for adult intervention. Part of your job as a parent is to be clear with your children about the importance of truth, and to insist on it at every opportunity.

Lying, especially about other people, can have great negative consequences. Reputations have been ruined by slander, families torn apart by vicious rumor. All children can provide personal recollections of occasions when someone said something about them that wasn't true. Ask your child to recall such a time. How did it make her feel? How did she feel about the other person? What (if anything) could she do to counteract what other people might have thought of her as a result of the falsehood? You might role-play with your child a situation in which a person is victimized by false gossip. Ask her to devise rules for behavior that might remind people how painful and harmful the experience can be.

"False witness" damages our faith in the system of law, justice, and public trust that helps hold our society together. An elected official accepting bribes, a business leader manipulating the legislative system for personal gain, a spiritual leader showing contempt for the ethical principles he preaches, all are instances of someone ignoring the Ninth Commandment. Examples with which we can teach are children are, unfortunately, available in the media almost every day.

The Tenth Commandment: Count Your Blessings

The key to satisfaction in life is hidden in the commandment, "You shall not covet": Don't desire something that belongs to someone else. The obsession that Americans call "keeping up with the Joneses" has probably sown more seeds of discontent than all the economic depressions and recessions in our history. The fact is, no matter how much of anything we have, we could always use more—more money, more possessions, more love, more space, more time, more pleasure—and this fact is one of humanity's greatest sources of dissatisfaction, frustration, jealousy, and anger.

The Tenth Commandment is a subtle program for fulfillment and happiness. To properly appreciate what we have in life, no matter what our age or state of development, is to discover what it takes to achieve satisfaction and joy in living. This appreciation is totally within our control and our children's, for it depends on only one thing—our attitude. Once our basic needs have been met, it isn't the circumstances of our lives that determine our happiness but the attitude we bring to these experiences. "You shall not covet" is a reminder that happiness comes from within.

Teaching your children to value the blessings and miracles that fill their lives is one of the most important lessons you could ever pass on to them. An easy way of getting this lesson across (try it on a long driving trip) is to have everyone in the family name the things that they cherish the most. What are their favorite "things" in their rooms, their homes, at school, and at work? Who are their favorite relatives and friends? What are their favorite places to visit or things to see and do? What skills, abilities, and personality traits are they most proud of?

After your family has listed all these blessings, talk about the children all over the world who have never experienced them and probably never will. The point isn't to feel guilty about having things that others don't; it's to train yourself and your children to recognize the gifts you have been given.

The Power of Moral Aphorisms

Do not stop with the Ten Commandments. There are many other ways to share your personal vision of ethical behavior with your family. For example, children appreciate short, easy-to-understand moral aphorisms that many of us learned at our own parents' knees, such as "God helps those who help themselves," or "Take your work seriously, not yourself." These moral aphorisms, or old adages, are a commonly accepted way to pass along to your children the best of our shared moral tradition, and can be useful ethical guidelines for specific situations. Everyone knows a few such sayings—words of wisdom that "My mother used to say," or "My father used to tell me." (My personal favorite comes from my grandfather: "Don't wish for fish, fish for fish.") One of the ways we learn about ethics is through these short, easily remembered moral aphorisms, and we are hardly aware that we've internalized them until we find ourselves drawing on one in a challenging moment. Take the Nichters, for example—the homeless family I mentioned at the beginning of this book who turned in the wallet full of cash. I doubt that "Honesty is the best policy," or any thought like it, was consciously in Pauline Nichter's mind as she went about her everyday life. But when she thought about what to do with that wallet, according to what she told reporters, she "heard" her mother's voice in her head, over and over, like a loop of tape, urging her to "do the right thing."

The Internal Parent Speaks in Aphorisms

We all have that internalized parent in our minds, reminding us with those short, pithy sayings to live in a caring, morally responsible way. Sometimes it's not a parent's voice that we hear but a grandparent's, a teacher's or someone else's. The point is that while moral modeling and complex verbal lessons are what transmit values, it's the moral aphorisms, catchy reminders of the behavior that supports these values, that spring into our consciousness at those moments when our ethics are being tested.

There are dozens of such moral adages—hundreds. A few are listed on the facing page on the chart **"Using Moral Aphorisms as Behavior Reminders."** Some we've all undoubtedly heard before; others new to me have been mentioned in my teacher-training workshops that I used to conduct.

Using Moral Aphorisms as Behavior Reminders

"Honesty is the best policy.

"Your word is your bond."

"Virtue is its own reward."

"If you don't have something nice to say, don't say anything at all."

"A trout in the pot is better than a salmon in the sea."

"You can catch more flies with honey than with vinegar."

"If you tell the truth, you don't have to remember what you said."

"With time and patience, the mulberry leaf becomes a silk gown."

"Laugh, and the world laughs with you."

"Even a small star shines in the darkness."

"It's always darkest just before the dawn."

"When life gives you lemons, make lemonade."

"A kind word turns away anger."

"Better poverty with love than riches with hate."

"If you don't open your mouth, no flies will get in."

"Boredom is a sin."

"Lost time is never found again."

"Gold and love affairs are hard to hide."

"Don't run after a man or a bus; there'll always be another one."

"Don't wish for fish, fish for fish."

Find appropriate moments to share familiar aphorisms with your children. These easy-to-understand expressions of challenging ideas can be useful guidelines for them in specific ethical situations. Do not forget, though, that all the powerful sayings in all the world's languages will not create ethical children unless they reflect behavior your children are experiencing through the everyday acts of their adult models—you.

Old adages can never take the place of personal example and conscious moral instruction. But it is satisfying to know that when your children are faced with moral decisions, they will hear the inner voice of conscience reminding them with an appropriate short saying to "do the right thing"—and the voice they hear will be your own.

The Ten Commandments—either in a religious or nonreligious context—and moral aphorisms, together with the suggestions in this book, are just a few of the hundreds of ethical ideas, values, and lessons you will want to share with your children. I have faith that with your personal commitment to raising children of character, you will be able to look back someday with pride and satisfaction at having left the world a better place to live.

Bibliography

Bettelheim, Bruno. *A Good Enough Parent.* New York: Vintage Books, 1988.

Brenner, Barbara. *Love and Discipline.* New York: Ballantine Books, 1983.

Church, Joseph, and Stone, Joseph, L. *Childhood and Adolescence: A Psychology of the Growing Person.* New York: Random House, 1979.

Clemes, H. and Bean, R. *Self-Esteem: The Key to Your Child's Well-Being.* New York: G. P. Putnam's Sons, 1981.

Coles, Robert. *The Moral Life of Children.* Boston: Houghton Mifflin Company, 1986.

Coopersmith, Stanley. *The Antecedents of Self-Esteem.* San Francisco: W. H. Freeman, 1967.

Curry, Nancy E., and Johnson, Carl N. *Beyond Self-Esteem: Developing a Genuine Sense of Human Value.* Washington, D.C.: National Association for the Education of Young Children, 1990.

Dinkmeyer, Don. "Teaching Responsibility, Developing Personal Accountability Through Natural and Logical Consequences." In *Experts Advise Parents,* edited by Eileen Shiff. New York: Delta Books, 1987, p. 183.

Dinkmeyer, Don, and McKay, Gary D. *Raising a Responsible Child.* New York: Fireside Books, 1973.

Dreikurs, R., and Grey, L. *A New Approach to Discipline: Logical Consequences.* New York: Hawthorne Books, 1968.

Dyer, Wayne W. *What Do You Really Want for Your Children?* New York: Avon Books, 1985.

Eimers, Robert, and Aitchison, Robert. *Effective Parents, Responsible Children.* New York: McGraw-Hill, 1977.

Fitzpatrick, Jean Grasso. *Something More.* New York: Viking Penguin, 1991.

Foster, Constance J. *Developing Responsibility in Children.* Chicago: Senior Research Associates, 1953.

Ginott, Haim G. *Between Parent and Child.* New York: Macmillan, 1965.

Glenn, Stephen H., and Nelson, Jane. *Raising Self-Reliant Children in a Self-Indulgent World.* Rockline, CA: Prima Publishing, 1989.

Grusec, Joan E., and Arnason, Lynn. "Consideration for Others: Approaches to Enhancing Altruism." In *The Young Child: Reviews of Research,* vol. 3, edited by Shirley G. Moore and Catherine R. Cooper. Washington, D.C.: National Association for the Education of Young Children, 1982, pp. 159-174.

Harris, James M. *You and Your Child's Self-Esteem.* New York: Warner Books, 1989.

Hendricks, Dr. Howard. "Family Happiness Is Homemade," *Family Concern,* vol. 13, no. 3 (March 1989).

Kohlberg, Lawrence. "Development of Moral Character and Moral Ideology." In *Review of Child Development and Personality,* vol. 1, edited by M. L. Hoffman and L. W. Hoffman. New York: Russell Sage, 1964.

Kurshan, Neil. *Raising Your Child to Be a Mensch.* New York: Atheneum, 1987.

LeShan, Eda. *The Parent's Guide to Everyday Problems.* New York: Atheneum, 1987.

Lickona, Thomas. *Raising Good Children.* New York: Bantam Books, 1983.

Marston, Stephanie. *The Magic of Encouragement.* New York: Pocket Books, 1990.

Magid, Ken and McKelvey, Carol. *High-Risk Children Without a Conscience.* New York: Bantam Books, 1987.

Nelson, Jane. *Positive Discipline.* Fair Oaks, CA: Sunrise Press, 1981.

Oppenheim, Joanne, Boegehold, Betty, and Brenner, Barbara. *Raising a Confident Child*. New York: Pantheon Books, 1984.

Peairs, Lillian, and Peairs, Richard H. *What Every Child Needs*. New York: Harper and Row, 1974.

Piaget, Jean. *The Moral Judgment of the Child*. New York: The Free Press, 1965.

Riley, Sue Spayth. *How to Generate Values in Young Children*. Washington, D.C.: National Association for the Education of Young Children, 1984.

Rosenthal, R., and Jacobson, L. *Pygmalion in the Classroom*. New York: Holt, Rinehart, and Winston, 1968.

Schulman, Michael, and Mekler, Eva. *Bringing Up a Moral Child*. Reading, MA: Addison-Wesley, 1985.

Segal, Julius, and Yahraes, Herbert. *A Child's Journey*. New York: McGraw-Hill, 1978.

Shiff, Eileen, Ed. *Experts Advise Parents*. New York: Delta Books, 1987.

Simon, Sidney. *I Am Lovable and Capable*. Niles, IL: Argus Communications, 1973.

Staub, Ervin. *Positive Social Behavior and Morality,* vol. 2. New York: Academic Press, 1979.

Wyckoff, Jerry L., and Unell, Barbara. *How to Discipline Your Six to Twelve Year Old. . . Without Losing Your Mind*. New York: Doubleday, 1991.

York, Phyllis, York David, and Wachtel, Ted. *Toughlove Solutions*. New York: Bantam Books, 1985.

Ziglar, Zig. *Raising Positive Kids in a Negative World*. New York: Ballantine Books, 1985.